FINALIST FOR THE NATIONAL BOOK AWARD

LONGLISTED FOR THE ANDREW CARNEGIE
MEDAL FOR EXCELLENCE IN NONFICTION

A MOST ANTICIPATED BOOK OF THE YEAR AT
*O, The Oprah Magazine*; *Forbes*; *Chicago Tribune*;
Electric Literature; BuzzFeed; Lit Hub;
The Millions; and Books Are Magic

"A gorgeous, brilliant book."
**–ELECTRIC LITERATURE**

"A personal, powerful, genre-bending
account of literary discovery."
**–BOOK RIOT**

"Following along with Shapland-as-detective is a
delight, and the mystery she sets out to solve is one
of those wicked unsolvables: how do we account for
the apertures in language, history, and identity?"
**–*LOS ANGELES REVIEW OF BOOKS***

"An intriguing, genre-blending debut."
**–*CHICAGO TRIBUNE***

"A beautifully written and hard-to-categorize
meditation on Carson McCullers and the hidden
literary history of queer women."
**–LIT HUB**

"A treatise on seeing yourself in someone else."
**–BUSTLE**

"Mind-bending!"

**—EMMA STRAUB, Books Are Magic**

"A mystery, a love story, a biography, several hearts on the page—I so loved this generous offering."

**—MOLLY MOORE, BookPeople**

"An exquisitely rendered map of discovery—of an icon, and of a self."

**—LAMBDA LITERARY**

"This book will change the way you think about the truth."

**—AUTOSTRADDLE**

"Shapland brings a sharp modern lens to her reading of McCullers' (and her own) life."

**—THE A.V. CLUB**

"Two books in one: an examination of a famous author whose narrative has been posthumously taken away from her, but also a vital memoir of Shapland's own experience as a queer woman looking for stories about people like her."

**—*HARPER'S BAZAAR***

"In lucid, distilled, honest prose, Jenn Shapland teaches us about McCullers, the desire for recognition, loneliness, the complexities of queer history, the seductions and resistances of the archive, and, all throughout, love."

**—MAGGIE NELSON**

"Gorgeous, symphonic, tender, and brilliant, *My Autobiography of Carson McCullers* is a monumental achievement. In this genre-bending work of nonfiction, Shapland brings the full weight of her intellect to bear on one of literature's most important questions: How do queer readers find the truth—and themselves—between the lines?"

**—CARMEN MARIA MACHADO**

"You do not need to be a queer woman, a lover of Carson McCullers' fiction, or interested in the mysterious junctures between our own lives and those of our favorite artists to love this book, but for those of us who *are* those things, Jenn Shapland's memoir is a particular trove of delights. My favorite biographies are full of historical literary gossip and interested in the shadow selves of public persons. My favorite memoirs are those that scrutinize the self as an unreliable source of narrative truth and the one we must nonetheless rely upon. *My Autobiography of Carson McCullers* manages to do all of this in earnest and honest and riveting vignettes. It is a detective story and a dissection of selfhood, a puzzle every piece of which pleased me as it clicked into place."

**—MELISSA FEBOS**

"You don't have to be a Carson McCullers fan to admire this remarkable book. It's a biography that's also a memoir, a story of obsession and longing. Captivating and trenchant and moving, Shapland's genre-mixing debut will stay with me a long time."

**–R.O. KWON**

"Jenn Shapland's *My Autobiography of Carson McCullers* is indeed part autobiography, part criticism, part memoir, and 100% human, reminding us of how books and writers can take our hands and lead us to uncover the mystery of our hearts. I've never read a book quite like it."

**–ANN HOOD**

# My Autobiography
of Carson McCullers

Published by Tin House, Portland, Oregon

Distributed by W. W. Norton & Company

Library of Congress Cataloging-in-Publication Data

Names: Shapland, Jenn, 1987- author.
Title: My autobiography of Carson McCullers / Jenn Shapland.
Description: Portland : Tin House, 2020. | Includes bibliographical references.
Identifiers: LCCN 2019031475 | ISBN 9781947793286 (hardcover) | ISBN 9781947793293 (ebook)
Subjects: LCSH: Shapland, Jenn, 1987- | Lesbians—United States—Biography. | McCullers, Carson, 1917-1967.
Classification: LCC HQ75.4.S53 A3 2020 | DDC 306.76/63092 [B]—dc23
LC record available at https://lccn.loc.gov/2019031475

First US Paperback Edition 2021
ISBN 978-1-951142-29-2 (paperback)
Printed in the USA
Interior design by Jakob Vala

www.tinhouse.com

"Queering the Archive" interview by Sarah Neilson, originally published in *Bookforum*, February 4, 2020.

# My Autobiography of Carson McCullers

a memoir by

# JENN SHAPLAND

 TIN HOUSE / Portland, Oregon

*For your Carson*

*In the recognition of loving*
*lies an answer to despair.*

—AUDRE LORDE,
*Zami: A New Spelling of My Name*

# Contents

# Author's Note

Due to copyright constraints, several documents, including letters, telegrams, and a set of transcripts made from Carson McCullers's recorded therapy sessions, have been referenced without direct quotations throughout this book.

# Question

Reeves asked Carson if she was a lesbian on the front porch of Carson's house on Stark Avenue, after everyone had gone to bed. I picture them on a swing, though I know for a fact that no such swing exists. Carson answered with a swift denial, wished aloud that she wasn't one, then expressed plain uncertainty.

I was the only patron in a small university archive in Columbus, Georgia, when I came across this exchange in a typed transcript dated March 1958. The transcript records Carson's fifth therapy session with Dr. Mary Mercer, whom she visited for help with writer's block. I read the question again. In her recollection, Carson told Reeves that she had loved a woman named Vera, another named Mary Tucker, but she wasn't sure what he referred to when he said lesbians. She asked him, as though lesbians might be a club that she could consider joining, or an unfamiliar species she might study: How do lesbians behave? Where do they live? How do they interact?

Despite Carson's status as maybe-lesbian, Reeves asked Carson when they would be married. She was nineteen.

# Articulation

Carson McCullers, when she is remembered, is remembered as a novelist who grew up in Columbus, Georgia, moved to New York in her twenties, and spent the rest of her life writing about misfits in the American South. Her characters are mute or too tall or black or queer and almost always lonely and out of place in a conservative small town that looks a lot like her own. In 1940, her first novel, *The Heart Is a Lonely Hunter*, brought her fame at twenty-three. Her books were made into films and Broadway plays. One of her best friends was Tennessee Williams—she called him Tenn—and she feuded with copycat Truman Capote for years. She married the same man, Reeves McCullers, twice, and is rumored to have chased after women. She was often drunk, chronically ill, and, like so many of her era, she died young. If you've heard of her, you've probably heard some version of this.

To tell her own story, a writer must make herself a character. To tell another person's story, a writer must make that person some version of herself, must find a way to inhabit her. This book takes place in the fluid distance between the writer and her subject, in the fashioning of a self, in all its permutations, on the page.

# Correspondence

I wasn't expecting love letters. The paper was browned with age and wrinkled at the edges. Annemarie's handwriting filled the page, bearing hard to the right and often spilling back up the left-hand margin with last additions. I read through clear Mylar sleeves, too intern-nervous to remove the pages from their housings.

> *April 10th, at night*
> *Carson, child, my beloved, you know that, leaving the day after tomorrow, feeling half-afraid and proud, leaving behind me all I care for, once again, and a wave of love—*

I looked up at the rows of manuscript boxes that surrounded me, mind humming, face flushed. Did that mean what I thought it meant? What did she mean, "love"? Instinctively, I listened for anyone who might be coming. Hearing only the ticking of the sliding electric shelves, I read on. To Carson, Annemarie recalled *talking as we did, you and I, at that*

*lunch time, you remember, at the corner near the Bedford Hotel,*
*with milk and bread and butter, ages ago.*

Four years before I visited the Georgia archives housing
Carson's transcribed therapy sessions, before I knew much
more of Carson than her name, I was an intern at the
Harry Ransom Center, a giant collection of writers' and
artists' books and papers on the University of Texas campus in Austin. The gig was a kind of coup: it got me out of
teaching for two years while I was a graduate student and
gave me unfettered access to the papers and belongings of
major writers.

On each day of my two years at the center, I came into the
shared intern office and answered queries from scholars
about their research from a stack of mail by the door. Most
were boring. About half of them were about either David
Foster Wallace or Norman Mailer. (My favorite find was a
series of letters one of Mailer's mistresses had written him
with the salutation—summing up my own feelings—*Dear
American Shithead.*) One day in early February 2012, a
scholar wrote asking for letters between Annemarie Clarac-
Schwarzenbach, whose name was utterly unfamiliar, and
Carson McCullers, whose book titles had always struck a
chord with me. *The Heart Is a Lonely Hunter.* Like, *same.* But
I'd never gotten around to reading any. Books seem to find
me when I'm ready for them, or else I abandon them. I took
the freight elevator down to the icy basement manuscript

room, pulled the correspondence folder—it was 29.4, I still recall—and started reading it right there in the stacks.

Annemarie's language in her letters to Carson is intimate, suggestive, or I read it that way. *You remember.* I had received letters like these. I had written letters like these to the women I'd loved. It was very little to go on, and yet I felt an utter certainty: Carson McCullers had loved women. Or at least, this woman had loved her. Immediately, without articulating a reason, I wanted to know everything about them both. I brought the folder upstairs to my shelf in the intern office, hurried to my three o'clock reference-desk shift, and started Googling. This was research, I rationalized; part of the job. Annemarie, I discovered, was a Swiss writer, photographer, silk heiress, and known lady-killer who spent time in New York in the 1930s and early '40s.

In folder 29.4 I found eight letters from Annemarie to Carson, but none of Carson's replies. One has the heading *On the Congo River, Sept. 1941*, another *On the boat, from Portuguese Angola to Lisbon.* After counting the pages for the scholar and replying to his request, I took the folder downstairs and tucked it back into its box. Later, I would keep stacks of Carson's books and manuscripts on my shelf in the office, but at that moment I didn't feel entitled to have these letters so nearby. I had, however, transcribed some of them into an email that I sent to myself. The scholar never ordered the scans.

Annemarie's handwriting is so small and insistent that the letters read long, though often they cover only the front and back sides of a single sheet. Her letters, like mine, are overwrought, wrung with feeling and a need to declare it in writing. In the first letter, it seems as if she is ending her relationship with Carson—gently, but firmly. She writes from Zurich, having already left the country:

> *Thank you forever . . . Carson, remember our moments of understanding, and how much I loved you. Don't forget the terrific obligation of work, be never seduced, write, and, darling, take care of yourself. As I will. (I wrote, in Sils. A few pages only, you would like them), and never forget, please, what has touched us deeply.*
>
> *Your Annemarie, with all my loving affection.*

The love she describes is bound up in writing, in creative work taken seriously by women. I think this part was just as striking to me as their romance, and now it reminds me of the feeling that Audre Lorde describes in her autobiography, *Zami*, when she first finds herself among a group of creative, queer women: "I felt myself pass beyond childhood, a woman connecting with other women in an intricate, complex, and ever-widening network of exchanging strengths." Like my own letters from my late teens and early twenties, Annemarie's letters are transmissions from one confused woman to another, an attempt to articulate a self she had not yet fully become. Rereading the letters I wrote during this period, I can hear myself still believing that one day soon my identity might resolve into something firm, fixed. I was waiting for my face to thin out, my hands to age. Other than my own, I had never read love letters between women before. For all Annemarie's and Carson's unfamiliarity to me, and their separation from me in time and space, I deeply understood them on the page.

I found the letters at the tail end of the major, slow-burning catastrophe of my twenties: never quite breaking up with my first love, a woman from Texas I'd met our freshman year of college in Vermont, after six closeted years together. In my second year of a six-year PhD program, I was already bored sick of academia. I didn't want to be a literary critic, couldn't stand the institutional hoops as I was jumping through them, and only six months into my internship I could tell I wasn't cut out to be an archivist. I didn't have the patience, and I spent too much time trying to solve mysteries of my own creation. I got an email out of the blue from one of my professors admiring my writing, and I jumped at what felt like validation. The praise continued, along with a barrage of poems and pressure to sleep with him, which I did, unsure exactly how I got there. My six-year relationship dissolved, and I moved out of our apartment. I was twenty-five and, when I wasn't drunk on a porch smoking angry cigarettes with my friends, I was exquisitely alone for the first time in my life in a new, over-priced studio apartment I couldn't afford. The dishwasher was full of roaches. The roaches were judging me. I was perplexed by my own behavior. I didn't know if I wanted to date women—I never really had; my first love and I publicly remained "roommates" for all those years—but, on the heels of manipulation, dating men seemed pretty dismal. Like most twenty-five-year-olds, I couldn't figure out what came next.

What came next was Carson.

I tried to tell a few people—coworkers, friends—about the letters, but I couldn't explain why they were so significant to me. "She dated a woman," they'd say. "So?" The years that followed were overtaken by my desire to understand the magnitude of this on-paper love. Within a week of find-ing the letters, I would chop my hair short. Within a year I would be more or less comfortably calling myself a lesbian for the first time. I would also catalog McCullers's collection of personal effects at the Ransom Center, her clothes and ob-jects that had made their way into the archive only to sit for years, unprocessed. Four years later I would live in Carson's childhood home in Columbus for a month, and soon after I would move from Austin to Santa Fe with my new love, Chelsea—we met as interns—abandoning my academic job search to finish a book about Carson. Retrospect redefines everything in its path, and I am as hesitant to ascribe steady narrative meaning to my own life as to any other's. But I suppose we could call those letters a turning point.

# The Soul's Particular Territories

Carson's therapy transcripts surfaced in 2014, after Dr. Mary Mercer's death, at the tiny third-floor archive of Columbus State University. I spent slow spring afternoons there in 2016, scanning and photocopying typo-strewn letters from Carson's post-stroke years, when her left arm was paralyzed and she typed with one finger. I read a copy of Carson's will, in which she leaves her former therapist one-third of everything, and lots of her letters to Mary, which are goofy and sweet: *I kiss your little foot*, she signs them, and addresses Mary as *heartchild*, one word. Many of these I photographed with my phone and texted immediately to Chelsea, with a cloud of exclamation points.

Martha, an older archivist with cropped blonde hair and wide-set eyes ringed by glasses, was in the midst of a heated conversation about mustard gas with other archive workers gathered around her computer when I walked through the door. I informed her I was there to work on Mary and Carson's friendship—that's what I called it. She scoffed performatively at the request, looking me up and down. Unfazed and already acquainted with her brand of aloofness, I handed her the long list of folders I wanted pulled. As I well know, archives can be grouchy, unapproachable places. It takes some effort on the part of a researcher to gain the staff's trust. They want to be sure you're serious. They guard a lot of secrets, the messy documents of often-messier lives. A few weeks later, I would think of these strained interactions as signs of Martha's, or the institution's, discomfort with the contents of the transcripts. I'm still not sure if that was just my queer researcher's paranoia talking.

Each of Carson's therapy transcripts is housed in a folder labeled "Experiment": "First Experiment," "Second Experiment." The transcripts themselves are maddeningly incomplete, sprinkled with ellipses and blanks that may or may not conceal additional details. Some begin or end midsentence. Carson speaks in all caps, interspersing poetry—her own and others'—with descriptions of her dreams, memories of childhood, and reflections on her life. It could seem especially violating to read the transcripts of a person's conversations with her therapist, as therapy ordinarily assumes confidentiality between counselor and patient. But the existence of these transcripts is anything but ordinary. Though they tell different versions of how this decision came about, both Mary and Carson describe these transcripts as an attempt at writing her autobiography.

Carson was skeptical of therapy at first and nervous about meeting Mary in 1958 at her practice in Nyack, New York, where Carson had lived on and off since 1944. Mary was forty-six, had been practicing psychiatry for over a decade, and had started a private practice in Nyack four years earlier. Carson's second autobiography, which, like the first, she never finished, was dictated from bed nine years after her therapy sessions and published posthumously in 1999 as *Illumination and Night Glare*. In it she writes that she feared "Dr. Mercer would be ugly, bossy, and try to invade my soul's particular territories." She was so worried she woke at three in the morning on the day of their first session. Egregiously early for the appointment, she walked up the path to the office with her cane, struggling to open the screen door, and saw Mary, who "was and is the most beautiful woman I've ever seen."

To approach her therapy as the writing of a memoir, Carson thought, was one of her real flashes of brilliance. At first, Mary was unsure and thought "it couldn't be done. It was contrary to the therapeutic 'contract.'" But eventually she was convinced. She told biographer Josyane Savigneau, "Against all reason and against the rules of my profession, I agreed to make the tapes—one copy for her and one copy for me—clearly stipulating that this material was not to be made public in its original form and would constitute only a resource for this book she planned to write." Mary got out the Dictaphone she used to record her correspondence and notes on her patients, and the two started recording right away. Carson didn't feel shy about what the tapes contained—she aimed to publish them. Their agreement is the reason the transcripts still exist at all, and I think it's also the reason I felt comfortable reading them, parsing them for subtext. Mary recalled hearing from Carson's friends that she was playing the therapy tapes "'for anyone and everyone,'" before Mary took them back from her.

In the late '50s, having lost her mother, whom everyone called Bebe, and a close friend, Carson was unable to write. Her current novel, which would eventually become *Clock Without Hands*, had her completely stuck. She was often alone; she didn't have a lot of money. She didn't feel that therapy with Mary was an expense she could afford, but after a few sessions she recognized its benefits. "I not only liked Dr. Mercer immediately," she writes, "I loved her, and just as important I knew I could trust her with my very soul. There was no difficulty in talking to her. All the rebellion and frustration of my life I handed over to her, for I knew that she knew what she was touching." If they could produce from the sessions an autobiography that Carson could sell, she would be able to justify the cost. While this sounds at once practical and ludicrous, I wonder if perhaps she was also looking for a narrative, trying to find a story she could tell in which she fit.

Carson is forty-one when the transcripts begin, and it's clear enough that she, a writer renowned for her psychological insight and emotional acuity on the page, is still at a loss as to how to articulate who she is. In April 1958, she tells Mary in a letter that her writing comes to her from a place of instinct, rather than analysis, and that she only comprehends what she writes after it is finished. When she first goes to see Mary, she feels so unable to interpret her own feelings and behaviors she compares herself to a person who has had a lobe of her brain surgically removed. So often a search for identity, for self-knowledge, is something we associate with youth. But in my own life, identity was slow to develop, and I didn't fully come into myself until my late twenties. Perhaps this is what I saw, from the start, in Carson: a familiarly protracted becoming.

Therapy has a lot in common with memoir: It's telling your story. I first visited a therapist the same spring I found the Annemarie letters. In the therapist's office, in the only dark corner of the fluorescent UT health center, I said over the gurgles of the cascading fountain on the table beside me, "I seem to have lost the narrative thread of my life." I said, "I just don't know what the narrative is anymore." What I was trying to say, I think, was that I didn't know how to talk my way through talk therapy without a story I could comprehend, a narrative logic into which I could insert my actions and my feelings. My behavior—the breakup, the roaches—felt illogical, self-destructive. And painfully naïve. "I was gawky and erratic and unmanageable to myself," as Jill Johnston, author of *Lesbian Nation*, describes her experience of coming to terms with her identity. (Or Eileen Myles: "I still liked men. I mean I was trying to.") That first therapist, a graduate student himself, didn't have much to offer me. I spent a good part of our session meditating— sitting in silence—at his suggestion.

My next therapist, E, was three floors down in a sunlit office she shared with a woo-kitsch aficionado. For the next four years I sat surrounded by crystals, framed Rumi quotes, and praying Buddhas as E helped me shape a new narrative, one that wasn't so strict and unforgiving. What I can tell you about my experience as a fledgling lesbian is that it took me a long time to accept and understand it, the identity, the word itself. Now I think of sexuality and identity, gender too, as processes of trial and error. You have to find what works for you. You need a narrative with room for messiness, one that can accommodate veering toward extremes.

As therapy, Carson and Mary's sessions were life-changing. Carson's quest for self-knowledge, which coincided with narrating her disastrous marriages and articulating her love for women, took place well into her adulthood. The tapes document a forty-one-year-old woman just figuring out who she is, dictating it in her soft southern purr. Carson's letters to Mary after each session are awash in the joy of self-revelation, among other joys. But Carson never published her therapy transcripts. After reading them over, she was heartbroken to find them garbled and indecipherable.

Yet I read them as if they were an unpublished manuscript, a draft tucked away in a drawer for a lifetime, only to find its way to a numbered folder in a numbered box in an archive. Carson may not have ultimately seen a book in them, but I do. I see the only story she ever wrote: a lonely misfit wrestles with her hidden self, unable to articulate her own longings.

According to Carson, after that first session, Mary invited her to lunch. They talked about books, though Mary had never read any of Carson's. Their post-session lunches, which continued through April 1958, were for Carson "the solace and high point" of the day. Insisting that theirs was a strictly doctor-patient relationship for the duration of Carson's therapy, Mary would later deny that these lunches ever took place.

# Derangement,
## or Why I Write

As I searched through the existing writings about Carson in my downtime at the Ransom Center, I found over and over that her relationship with Annemarie was sidelined or left out of a story about her and Reeves. It doesn't seem as if these are, for the most part, acts of outright censorship on the part of biographers or the people they interviewed. Many of the details of Carson's lesbian life are right there, in plain sight. It's just that they are housed within another narrative: the straight narrative, the one in which inexplicable crushes on and friendships with women surface briefly within the confines of an otherwise "normal" life. In the published biographies, Annemarie is just a one-sided obsession. ("Carson loved Annemarie far more than Annemarie could ever requite," according to Virginia Spencer Carr's *The Lonely Hunter*, and "Annemarie did not return Carson's enthusiasm," writes Sherill Tippins in *February House*.) The more I read, the more it seemed that all of her profound emotional relationships with women were either dismissed or ridiculed. Mary becomes, in these retellings, some kind of nursemaid to a sickly, emotionally flatulent Carson, and the other significant women in Carson's life—Mary Tucker, Elizabeth Ames, Janet Flanner, Natalia Danesi Murray, Marielle Bancou, Gypsy Rose Lee, Jane Bowles—all become minor characters.

Yet as I read and reread her letters and conversations with Mary, I found a fuller version of Carson's life revealed through her relationships. I am more convinced than ever that we are shards of others. Through her relationships with other women, I can trace the evidence of Carson's becoming, as a woman, as a lesbian, and as a writer. There are so many crushes in a lifetime, so many friendships that mix desiring-to-have with wanting-to-be. It's the combination of wants that makes these longings confusing, dangerous, and queer. There is a desire to know that is already knowing, a curiosity for what you deep down recognize, a lust for what you are or could be. Writer Richard Lawson describes it as "the muddied confusion over whether you want to be someone's companion or if you want to step inside their skin, to inhabit the world as they do."

It is by no means easy to track or trace relationships between women, past or present. Women's relationships with other women are often disguised: by well-documented marriages to men, by a cultural refusal to see what is in full view or even to believe such relationships exist. In a world built by and for men and their pursuits, a woman who loves women does not register—and is not registered, i.e., written down. Reasons for this layer one upon the other: a lesbian purposely hides her identity and remains closeted. A lesbian refuses to call herself a lesbian, disidentifying from the term and its associations for reasons personal or political. A woman does not know she is a lesbian—because she does not ever have a relationship with another woman, or because she is not aware that the relationships she engages in could be called lesbian. I didn't call myself one for several years: hence the "roommate." Or, as in Carson's case, her own self-understanding and identification are difficult to determine due to the efforts of those who outlived her and pushed her into the closet.

It was her retroactive closeting by peers and biographers that I found most disturbing. I took it personally. I began to feel unreal, deranged. If Carson was not a lesbian, if none of these women were lesbians, according to history, if indeed there hardly is a lesbian history, do I exist?

Rather than name or talk about Carson's formative loves and friendships with women, the biographies cast them aside in favor of an account of her "tortured" relationship with Reeves McCullers, the man she married and unmarried twice in her life. The straight narrative is given the benefit of the doubt, and writers feel comfortable filling in the blanks to create a great and desperate love story out of what looks, on my reading, like a series of manipulations of a woman struggling to name her own desires. Perhaps it isn't even as sinister as knowingly replacing one narrative with another. Maybe it's just that the stories of her relationships with women are partial, hard to compile. To piece them together, you have to read like a queer person, like someone who knows what it's like to be closeted, and who knows how to look for reflections of your own experience in even the most unlikely places.

There are many ways to interpret a life. But what if we choose the most probable scenario, the path of least resistance, instead of trying to talk our way out of what seems evident, instead of trying to explain away the obvious? Lesbian historian Emily Hamer writes, "We know that they were lesbians because this is the best explanation of their lives. . . . The standard of visibility is not a universal prerequisite for knowledge. We cannot see electricity but we know that electricity exists because electricity is the best explanation of why moving a light switch leads to the illumination of a light bulb."

Savigneau doubts whether Carson ever experienced sexual desires, period, "romantic obsessions" with certain women aside. She is, unfortunately, not alone in this opinion. She writes, "The labels *lesbian* and *bisexual* have been used by those who denigrate any form of marginality to distance themselves from Carson McCullers by categorizing her as an 'abnormal artist.' They have also been used by partisans of homosexuality—both male and female—who would appropriate the writer for their cause." Savigneau's biography came out in English in 2001. Her description positions me as a "partisan of homosexuality" seeking to "appropriate" Carson's story for my "cause." And perhaps I am.

# Caves

After finding the therapy transcripts, I drove back to Carson's house through a cloud of yellow-green pollen from trees in heavy flower. I had come to Columbus to be alone, to experience McCullers's town and home, thinking that perhaps the buildings themselves, the trees, the streets would reveal what I couldn't find in published writings about her. The foundation that manages Carson's house had offered me a chance to stay there, and though the timing wasn't perfect—I was in my last semester of graduate school and hadn't finished the dissertation I'd be defending in a month—this residency seemed too good to pass up. I was also in the flush of new love and couldn't believe I was choosing to be alone in Georgia for four weeks.

I hadn't quite grasped that I would be living in a museum. When I arrived at the Stark Avenue house and glanced around at its closed floral curtains soaked in dust, and its sun-faded fan-art paintings of Carson's face, I panicked. I suddenly felt alone, scared, unsure why I'd come all the way here and planned to stay a month. What connection did I even have to Carson, really? I'd read so much about her, but all I knew of her in three dimensions were the objects of hers I'd found at the Ransom Center: the shape of her feet in wool knee-high socks, the patina of her skin on an old cigarette lighter. Here she felt like a whole person I could neither see nor touch. I became afraid that, in the very process of trying to know her, I would somehow change her. Perhaps I had been expecting her to keep me company. But, needless to say, Carson wasn't there.

Nor was she in any of the books I'd been devouring about her since I'd read the Annemarie letters. This project, this hunt for the Carson of Annemarie's letters, had seemed at a distance like a useful escape from my dissertation and from the bleak academic job market. Now that I was padding around her house in socks, surrounded by her things, I felt daunted. I thought I would use my own life as a writer, as a queer person, as a chronically ill person, to tell Carson's untold story. But after reading the transcripts, I realized that she'd already told it.

I called Chelsea and informed her I wasn't going to be able to stick it out. All the rooms were dark, the house strange and musty. "What am I," I demanded, "the living dead?" It was late February 2016, and too many of the neighboring lawns bore signs for nightmare right-wing candidates. Chelsea talked me down, reminded me that it always takes me a few beats to get used to a new space. I went to the grocery store. I bought orange lilies and a basil plant and things to eat. When I woke the next morning, the kitchen glowed with sunlight. The green things helped remind me that I, too, was a living thing. I was the one bringing life to this project. Lying in bed in the downstairs library, a wood-paneled, carpeted addition to the house I called my cave, I read an interview with Myles that offers writing, self-exposure or self-representation, as an antidote to—or an action of—loneliness: "You tell it cause you're lonely—you're the only person *inside* that life." I wrote in my journal, "I always have to find my own way into things. Whatever is here I will make it myself from scratch. I will find it and assemble it or unbuild it."

Within a few days, I started taking walks in the neighborhood. There's a park a few blocks down the hill called Little Wildwood with huge trees and a sizable stone pyramid I assumed was a monument. When I crossed the park and approached the pyramid, I found no inscription or explanation for it, a glaring metaphor for the blankness I was feeling. The neighborhood is a cluster of old houses, some of them mansions, though not Carson's. It reminded me of my hometown, a wealthy suburb on the north shore of Chicago where I never quite fit in. When I first read Carson's fiction, sitting behind various desks in the Ransom Center, I felt an immediate connection to the small southern towns where her characters, often adolescents, strongly sense their own unbelonging and isolation. The suburbs of the Midwest of my childhood in the 1980s and '90s resemble Columbus in their fondness for gossip, their sense of tradition, their prizing of normalcy at all costs (not to mention their tacit racism and homophobia). I didn't meet, and rarely saw, any of the neighbors while I was in Columbus, though I frequently wondered what they thought of me strolling their empty streets, reading on the front porch, where by all appearances no one had sat in years. Outsiderness is a stance.

# Chick-fil-A

The Chick-fil-A was how I knew where to turn for Carson's house, which is green with another green house next door, and a code to get inside, and a feeling of dead dust. Her neighborhood, which used to perch on the rural outskirts of Columbus, now borders an excruciatingly typical main thoroughfare lined with fast food, a Rite Aid and a Walgreens, and a Circle K. I have never eaten Chick-fil-A, for obvious political reasons, but the drive-thru lane was always overflowing and blocking the turn for Stark Avenue. Instead, one night I ordered a pizza, and the delivery guy showed up on Carson's porch and asked, "Do you live here?"

"Yes," I said immediately, concerned that his handing over the pizza depended on a correct answer. "Well, sort of."

The pizza man told me he goes by the place every day, he grew up nearby, and the historic registry sign out front made him think it was a museum.

"It is," I told him, and he eyeballed me. I was thrilled by this awkward encounter, my first conversation with a person in days, and, pizza in hand, I closed the door behind him, sad to see him go. I wanted to play ghost a little longer.

# Tree Houses and
# Telephone Booths

The house sits back from the street and is so unassuming I almost passed by it when I arrived. It has dark-green clapboards, cream window trim, and white stucco columns, with black wrought-iron railings flanking the steps to the porch. All of the windows are blanked out from within by closed curtains.

Carson wasn't born in this house, but downtown on Thirteenth Street. The family moved to the suburbs when she was eight. As a child, Carson and her brother hid out in their backyard tree house, which had a pulley to bring up snacks they requested from the cook using an "elaborate signal system." She doesn't describe herself as unhappy, though she adds, "Years later when I was troubled I would still take refuge in that same tree house." The snack-pulley detail is significant, as Carson writes that while she was growing up, her family never had dessert. "Perhaps that was because mother knew that every morning I would go to King's grocery store and buy six bars of chocolate before

I went to school. I would munch on these all during the day and I cannot recall how many times I was sent out of the room for eating in class." In other words, Carson took care of herself. Mary tried to interpret this in their sessions: "What about the meaning of desserts and sweets in life? They are the things one earns only after eating one's vegetables. And you needed the sweets because they substituted for love?" Carson's autobiography doesn't include many of the usual details about school or friendships with peers, but she talks about food a *lot*. And she talks about music. "My childhood was not lonely," she writes in *Illumination*, "because when I was five years old in 1922, my Daddy bought a piano."

Carson also found company in books. Her longtime favorite was the autobiography of dancer Isadora Duncan, *My Life*. "When I was fourteen years old, the great love of my life, which influenced the whole family, was Isadora Duncan," she writes. She tried to start a dance company and informed her father that the family would be moving abroad to support her dancing dreams, which were short-lived. As a kid, Carson was frequently ill, with almost yearly bouts of pneumonia, and missed a lot of school. Her closest friends were adults: aunts and grandmothers were significant early on, and her nannies and maids all make appearances in *Illumination*—black women role models even if, in the 1920s small-town South, they were household servants. In therapy she calls her piano instructor, Mary Tucker, one of her first loves and describes her as a kind of personal deity. For years, she took lessons at Tucker's house every Saturday and planned to be a musician, attending high school only sporadically and spending most of her time on music. Cue the song of the queer, creative childhood, the telltale signs of growing up isolated, independent, and artistic in a conservative place. She writes, "I yearned for one particular thing; to get away from Columbus and to make my mark in the world."

In 1934, Carson escaped to New York, sailing from Savannah at seventeen. "For the first time I saw the ocean," she writes, "and, later, marvel of marvels, I saw snow." Beyond reaching the city, she didn't have much of a plan. Though she'd set her sights on Juilliard, one way or another (either she determined her father, a watch repairman, couldn't afford it, as she has it in *Illumination*, or she spent or gave away her tuition en route—to a prostitute who offered to show her to the subway, if you ask Tenn) she decided to pursue writing instead of music. On switching "professions" from musician to writer, she notes, "That was something I could do at home, and I wrote every morning." Given her health, working at home seemed to Carson like a logical idea.

Carson wasn't comfortable in New York at first. Her roommate, a student at Columbia, had a boyfriend and was never home. On her way back to the room one day, a man came up the stairs behind Carson. He "tried to put his arms around me but I pushed him away so violently that he ricocheted against the wall," she recalls. "So I was stuck there in that lonely room with a sense of menace and a fear of strange men. [In the daytime I'd go to Macy's and just sit in the telephone booth where I knew I was safe. Then back to the horror of a sleepless night.]" She moved to women's group housing at the Parnassus Club, then the Three Arts Club, and found sleep more easily surrounded by other creative women. I flashed back to my own six-month stint in New York, a semester at NYU my sophomore year of college, when I thought I'd finally find my people, my life, and everything I wanted that had yet to surface at my small, preppy Vermont school. Instead, I showed up in the city in Birkenstocks and knew immediately that I was on my own. I spent all my days alone in coffee shops and on benches and taking long, slow walks. I was queer but closeted. I mailed arduous letters to my girlfriend, abroad in Athens. I spent a lot of time at the Strand. I remember it as the loneliest time of my life.

Carson had a series of jobs while she lived in the city: typist, waitress, piano player for dance classes, comics editor. She would often wake up at four or five in the morning to fulfill her daily writing quota. Whatever she wrote that she didn't like, she destroyed, a practice that continued all her life. In *Illumination,* she claims she never had a job she wasn't fired from, "a perfect record." She began showing

apartments for a real estate agent, Mrs. Louise B. Field.
"The main part of the job, I remember, was getting sour
cream for Mrs. Field, which she would eat with a long ice
tea spoon. But once, when I was reading Proust behind the
ledger and got involved in a long Proustian sentence, Mrs.
Field caught me." Fired again, her boss informed her she
would "never amount to anything in this world." I'm familiar with reading on the job. Chelsea claims that I spent
the entire two years I worked at the Ransom Center sitting
outside on a bench in the courtyard, reading in the sun. As
I recall it, I was usually reading inside the building. After I
found the Annemarie letters, I was reading all the center's
first-edition copies of Carson's novels, trying to remember
not to fold down the corners of the pages.

# *That* Girl

Carson spent summers in Columbus with her new friend Edwin D. Peacock, a musician she had met at a Rachmaninoff concert who "introduced [her] to Marx and Engels" at seventeen. The books he gave her provided new language in which to parse the injustice she had sensed as a child upon seeing black people rooting through trash cans during the Depression. In her words, "I had realized . . . that there was something fearful and wrong with the world, but I had not in any way thought of it intellectually" prior to Edwin. Of their relationship, she clarifies, "I was not 'in love,' but it was a real friendship, which has indeed lasted throughout all my life." Edwin later opened a bookstore in Charleston, South Carolina, with his partner, John Zeigler, and Carson would visit them in the summer at the beach. There are great photos of Carson surrounded by a throng of men in teeny bathing suits. Gay men formed Carson's core social circle in many phases of her life. I wonder if gay men were easier to spot and befriend, or more prevalent among groups of writers in the 1930s, '40s, and '50s than lesbians. In the 1950s, "meeting other lesbians was very difficult," Lorde writes in *Zami*. Regardless of the reason, Carson was most at home with queer friends from the time she was a teenager.

During her second year in New York, enrolled in writing courses with Dorothy Scarborough and Helen Rose Hull at Columbia University, Carson got a letter from Edwin, who wanted to introduce her to his new friend, Reeves McCullers, an army clerk at Fort Benning in Georgia. According to Carson, Reeves was "the best looking man I had ever seen," and "a liberal, which was important, to my mind, in a backward Southern community." When Carson came home again for the summer, she, Edwin, and Reeves were inseparable. They were one of a series of Carson's chosen families, and they spent whole days together. To her neighbors in Columbus, Carson was different on her return than the old Carson they knew before she left for New York. Now she chain-smoked and typed all day on the typewriter her father had given her, and the neighbors started to talk. They considered her to have "radical opinions." After Carson fell off a horse at Fort Benning and "turned up braless" at the hospital, writer Elizabeth McCracken recounts in the *Oxford American*, the mother of an editor at the local paper subsequently responded to any mention of Carson: "'Oh *that* girl . . . Well . . . She didn't wear a brassiere.'"

The following summer, she took a workshop with Whit Burnett, the editor of *Story* magazine, who would publish her first short story "Wunderkind" in 1936. In the winter, Carson came down with a fever, which was thought to be tuberculosis. Decades later, her doctor would determine that this had been rheumatic fever, which had damaged her heart and would cause her life-defining strokes and the paralysis of her left arm. While she was in Columbus recovering, Sylvia Chatfield Bates, her NYU writing teacher, sent her word of a first novel contest being held by Houghton Mifflin, and Carson submitted an outline called "The Mute," a story about a deaf-mute man, John Singer, and his deaf-mute "friend" and roommate, Spiros Antonapoulos. In the preface to her outline—which Carlos Dews includes in the published version of *Illumination*—Carson writes, "Singer's love for Antonapoulos threads through the whole book from the first page until the very end. No part of Singer is left untouched by this love and when they are separated his life is meaningless and he is only marking time until he can be with his friend again. Yet the four people who count themselves as Singer's friends know nothing about Antonapoulos at all until the book is nearly ended." This outline, which won the contest, would become *The Heart Is a Lonely Hunter*. Like her later works *Reflections in a Golden Eye*, *Clock Without Hands*, and "The Jockey," Carson's first novel boldly explores a hidden relationship between two men without naming or defining it.

# Qualifications

Eleanor Roosevelt crossed the aisle at the 1961 Broadway premiere of Tennessee Williams's *The Night of the Iguana* to introduce herself to Carson, who was sitting with the playwright and his mother. Jordan Massee, Carson's gay BFF and distant cousin, whom she called Boots, described this as "a tribute that meant more to Carson than the Pulitzer Prize." Roosevelt, it was later revealed, had a long and well-documented lesbian relationship with a reporter named Lorena Hickok, which Susan Quinn unearthed and devoted nearly four hundred pages to in her biography *Eleanor and Hick*. "Yet," Quinn writes,

> I still encounter people who are reluctant to believe that Eleanor Roosevelt was passionately involved with another woman. . . . I suspect that people react this way because they have a fixed idea of Eleanor Roosevelt, with her flowered hat and her purse and her sensible shoes, slightly bent forward as she marches off to make the world a better place. *That*

Eleanor Roosevelt dwells in a world that transcends
all the longings, hurts and excitements of passion.
But that public persona masked the real Eleanor—
as her letters to Hick make abundantly clear.

The easy joke here: But aren't lesbians supposed to *love*
sensible shoes? However, if we stop short of making lesbians a joke for once, and take them seriously as people, as
women, we find individuals who choose to make their lives
and their bodies sites for their politics and their feminism.
I would like to celebrate this choice by finding its every nu-
ance and expression.

The first researcher who had access to Eleanor and Hick's letters, (which were opened to the public ten years after Hick's
death, as she had stipulated), a woman named Doris Faber,
was appalled and insisted that the FDR library restrict the
materials from public access. Stumbling upon their secret,
she wanted it locked back up, Hick's own wishes be damned.
In her book *The Life of Lorena Hickok: E. R.'s Friend*, Faber turned their romance into a "friendship," and even then
people came after her for so much as suggesting any kind
of intimacy, even platonic, between Roosevelt and another
woman. It seems Faber could hardly imagine such a thing.
Nonetheless, these critics were distressed by the acknowl-
edgment of even a close friendship between women. In the
context of outright censorship of women's relationships, it
only makes sense that Carson's story would be repackaged

as a straight narrative. This ongoing suppression of details is even more troublesome given the burden of proof placed on queer relationships, both historical and present day: if it can't be proved with direct evidence of sexual intimacy, it never happened. And if you're looking for evidence, it won't ever be published.

I never expected to find any confirmation of Carson's relationship with Mary Mercer, though I had my own reasons to suspect it. While she was alive, Mary didn't breathe a word. In the years following Carson's death, Mary was unwilling—unable—to speak openly with anyone about her. No one had access to the therapy transcripts or Carson's letters to Mary, which Mary held back from the archive until her death in 2013. She refused biographers permission to use her letters (those that existed). Her censorship was thorough. When the Duke University Archives asked for her letters to Mary Tucker, Carson's childhood piano teacher, with whom she developed a friendship after Carson died, Mary told Mary Tucker in a letter, "Destroy them."

It is strange to apply the expectations of discovery and evidence to a person's life, let alone a person's love life. As I read and researched Carson, I learned that evidence itself is slippery, and discoveries are never final. They shift as more voices, more sources are added to the mix. They shift according to the mood of the biographer or the critic, and according to my own mood, and according to the mood of the weather on the day I'm reading. I didn't trust the discovery of Carson's relationship with Mary that I found in the transcripts, in part because I suddenly didn't trust myself as a reader. If Carson was a lesbian, and if her relationships bore that out, wouldn't *someone* already have said so? Wouldn't it be known beyond rumors in the queer community? It was a real mind-fuck, the back-and-forth between scanning indexes of heavily researched biographies that do not contain the words "gay" or "lesbian" or "homosexual" and reading Carson's adamant descriptions of her own feelings and experiences. I also realized on some level that I was a confused queer person looking to Carson as a role model—I looked to everyone I met as a role model; I was in my midtwenties—and so I must have been reading into her queerness, seeing what I wanted to see. I must have been a partisan of the gay agenda. Already I was suspicious of my own desire for "proof."

In the introduction to his notes on her life, Boots writes, "I knew Carson too long and too well to be removed completely from the story of her life . . . but just what my role was, and how important, is not for me to decide. I am hardly qualified to write a biography of Carson McCullers."

I am hardly qualified to write a biography of Carson McCullers. Who am I to her? I slid my arms up the sleeves of her long lime-green wool coat, I folded her nightgowns, I labeled her socks. I made biscuits in the kitchen of her childhood home and I walked in the park where she used to play by herself. I have read enough biographies to know, in no uncertain terms, that they are built of artifice and lies. I am not a fiction writer, and this is not a biography.

Biographers usually seek to fill in gaps, to add narrative to strict chronology, to render a person's life so that it reads like a nineteenth-century novel. But Carson's is not an unwritten story. Rather, it is a story that has been written over, revised, and adjusted to suit various people's needs. The more I read and researched, the more I began to question the versions of her life that exist and continue to circulate. I began to feel that someone—several someones—had put the jigsaw puzzle together all wrong, to form a picture of Carson that didn't match the one I recognized. First, I had to take the puzzle apart and find all the faulty links. Then I began to reassemble it, a six-year process that took me from Austin, Texas, to Columbus, Georgia, to Saratoga Springs, New York, following leads and trying to fit the pieces together without knowing what the final version—my Carson—would look like. I'm still not sure how to know if I am done. It is customary when writing a biography to talk to as many people who personally knew the subject as possible, but I instinctively avoided this. I didn't want to meet anyone. I didn't want to encounter another person who might try to put the pieces back their own way, who would tell me where the pieces go. I wanted only the pieces in her words, and time.

Carson's biographies, both the full-length books and the life summaries that get rehashed whenever she is mentioned in print, take discrete forms. There is Carson the prodigy, the wunderkind, a shy small-town girl who bumbles her way to literary stardom. There's Carson the drunk, sloppy and salty and probably exaggerating. And Carson the needy, ailing woman who is a burden to everyone who gets close to her. Carson the desperate, chasing down women and men; and Carson the manipulator, seducing and using others. Carson called herself "a bit of a holy terror" and said she was writing her autobiography to explain how her early success and her chronic illness "nearly destroyed" her. None of these is my Carson.

"I never thought 'my Jane' might approximate the 'real Jane'; I never even had designs on such a thing," Maggie Nelson writes of her aunt, Jane Mixer, about whom she published two books. Reading these lines is deeply comforting to me, for what claim can I possibly make on a "real" Carson? She died twenty years before I was born. She was born seventy years before I was, on February 19, 1917. My birthday is the sixteenth. At most I can claim shared sun signs, and even that depends on your choice of astrological calendar. When I arrived at her childhood home a few weeks after my twenty-ninth birthday, when I had insisted to everyone who would listen that I was actually *thirty*, I found a partially eaten ninety-ninth birthday cake for Carson, with her face silk-screened onto the frosting, inhabiting the entire bottom shelf of the fridge. Apart from forlorn condiments and leftover bottles of cheap wine, the cake was the fridge's sole occupant. The director of the Mc-Cullers Center told me, cordially, that I should help myself. Instead I squeezed my groceries in around the cake for several weeks, trying not to touch it, until an employee of the center arrived early to set up for an event and threw the whole thing into the trash can outside.

Nelson writes, "But whoever 'my Jane' was, she had certainly been alive with me, for me, for some time." Is my Carson alive? What would that mean? I think of her more as a poltergeist, able to inhabit the objects that I encounter, charging them with something close to, but not quite, life.

I am trying to resurrect the exact moment of each of my subtle revelations about Carson: the white archival gloves holding up photographs by a corner, the lens of the camera, the air in the room, the glare of the overhead lights. Carson in a pinstriped suit and tall argyle socks, sitting at a piano. Carson lounging in the grass as a kid, in huge baggy shorts and her dad's tie. How I long to preserve my first glimpses of these images, these things. All the while aware that as I preserve them in writing, I am removing older versions, overriding them, inevitably losing information—akin to what digital-era archivists, unknowing poets, call "lossiness."

# A Free Love

When Reeves first tried to hold Carson's hand, she was appalled. She went home and told her father about it, insisting that such a step would be disruptive to their friendship. She repeated the same thing to Reeves when he tried to kiss her the next time they were out driving. But Reeves was determined. All summer Reeves had been borrowing Edwin's bike to ride with Carson out to, of all places, a vacant Girl Scout camp, stopping for Cokes and eating picnics made by Bebe and swimming and playing chess. Reeves was getting ready to leave for New York, and apparently he wanted more from Carson than just a picnic. As she remembers it, the very next time he came to see her, post-attempted kiss, he asked her if she was a lesbian as they sat on the porch of the house on Stark Avenue, where I perched in 2016 listening to the rain night after night, hoping the pollen footprints would wash away.

I'm piecing together these early days from the therapy transcripts, trying to understand how they fit with the other timelines, other versions I have read. Carson tells Mary that, that night, Reeves kissed her as Baudelaire describes kissing his mistress. Leave it to Carson to bring in some French poet at the crucial moment. No wonder so many of her biographers figure she never had sex. Afterward, whatever happened, Reeves asked Carson if she enjoyed it. Carson says she believes she liked it, though she was terrified her parents might come out and catch them in flagrante. He asked her again, and this time she said that indeed, she did enjoy it. Carson's retelling of this event is ambivalent. She is distracted by the threat of being caught, unsure of her own feelings, and Reeves is persistent, pressuring. He tells her it doesn't matter whether or not she's a lesbian because he loves her, and then changes the subject to setting a wedding date. A year later they married. Carson's articulated feelings, her uncertainty about whether or not she's a lesbian, are somehow totally worthless here.

After Edna St. Vincent Millay graduated from Vassar, where she had "smashes" on many a female classmate, she tried to continue to live as a lesbian in Greenwich Village in the 1920s. Bohemians, historian Lillian Faderman writes, were rapidly accepting bisexuality as another means to flout Victorian sensibilities and the previous century's utter denial of women's sexual autonomy. With the new writings of the sexologists in hand, women were recognizing that they had desires and that other women could fulfill them. Yet for Millay, who had gone by "Vincent" during her college years, exclusively loving women was not accepted, even by her progressive bisexual community in the Village. A man named Floyd Dell pressured her to go to bed with him, though "she was obviously ambivalent, insisting they remain fully clothed and refusing to have intercourse." As to her reluctance, Dell told her, "'I know your secret . . . You are still a virgin. You have merely had homosexual affairs with girls in college.'" This line of reasoning, that women's relationships with other women (especially in college) do not count as full, mature sexual experiences, continues to this day. Dell writes in his memoir that he felt it was his "'duty to rescue her'" from her lesbian proclivities. He was unsuccessful in his mission.

Carson tells Mary about a conversation she had with her parents before marrying Reeves at age twenty, an anecdote she later included in the opening of *Illumination.* She writes, "When I asked my mother about sex she asked me to come behind the holly tree & said with her sublime simplicity, 'Sex, my darling, takes place where you sit down.' I was therefore forced to read sex textbooks, which made it seem so very dull, as well as incredible." Carson insisted that she live with Reeves before they married, telling her parents, "I don't want to marry any man unless I know what sex is about . . . I want to know what I'm contracting with." About her first sexual encounter with Reeves, she notes, "the sexual experience was not like D. H. Lawrence. No grand explosions or colored lights." She explained to her parents that she longed to have the freedom and free love of Isadora Duncan, and not to be confined by marriage or convention. This is a classic Carson moment in her irreverence, her unwillingness to accept her parents' shock as a tolerable reaction. But it also gives us a clue to her own ideas about sexuality and a sense of continuity that she had identified in herself since adolescence. She tells Mary that she wanted to be at liberty to love whomever she wanted, as though such freedom, such fluidity, could constitute an identity. For Carson, I think it does.

The summer before fifth grade, I found a biography of Zelda Fitzgerald, Nancy Milford's *Zelda*, on the second floor of the local library, in the nonfiction section I'd only recently discovered. The skylights made it the brightest part of the building. I sat down on a plastic stool between the shelves and started reading. I devoured the book that summer. I was fascinated. I don't know why I picked it up, though the cover is striking: the title in white script on a background of peacock feathers, a photo of Zelda on the back cover at age thirty-one, sitting on a trunk in what appears to be an attic, in a polo shirt, a tutu, and pointe shoes. She was unprecedented. The book itself was bright green, I could see under the jacket, and the endpapers were an outrageous purple. Milford's Zelda—audacious, creative, fiercely independent in her thinking—was my new junior high idol. Zelda loved and admired Isadora Duncan, so I did, too. It's sad to realize now that Zelda Fitzgerald was the closest thing I had growing up to a lesbian role model. In the pages of her biography, I saw the outlines of who I might become. Looking back at the book, which I found a used copy of in my twenties, I am more intrigued by the overlap between myself and Milford, the biographer, whose prologue begins, "When I was young in the Midwest and had dreams of my own."

Alone in my red Civic for two days as I drove from central Texas to Carson's house in 2016, I passed through Montgomery, Alabama, and though I was only a few hours from my destination, I decided to visit what I thought was Zelda's childhood home, which had been made into a museum. I hadn't read *Zelda* since I was young, but I remembered the stories of her glamorous southern upbringing, so foreign and yet familiar to me as a child of the snobbish Midwest. I walked up the garden path, let myself in the front door, and found myself in a museum devoted not to Zelda but to her husband and his work. In the back room hung Zelda's flamboyant watercolor paper dolls, made for her daughter, Scottie, alongside some of her paintings. But otherwise, the house told the story of her husband's life and writing. Her husband, who, as Milford's biography taught me, stole her ideas for his fiction. Her husband, who destroyed her work. Who institutionalized her.

The stories of women are paved over by others' narratives so often that we rarely get to hear about how things went from their perspectives, from the inside. Constant revision is required of queer women trying to navigate and self-actualize in straight spaces. I imagine this was what Carson found in Duncan's book. In *My Life*, Duncan writes, "No woman has ever told the whole truth of her life. The autobiographies of the most famous women are a series of accounts of the outward existence, of petty details and anecdotes which give no realization of their real life. For the great moments of joy or agony they remain strangely silent."

Carson and Reeves married in the living room of her parents' house in 1937, when she was twenty. Of the wedding, which only her family, Boots, and Edwin attended, Boots "insisted I was married in a green velvet gown and oxfords," Carson writes. "Could be? I can't remember."

# Windows

If biography is peering through the windows of someone's house and describing what you see—or, less generously, as Janet Malcolm has it, if the biographer "is like the professional burglar, breaking into a house, rifling through certain drawers that he has good reason to think contain the jewelry and the money, and triumphantly bearing his loot away"—memoir is peeking into the windows of your own life. A voyeurism of the self. An interior looting. Your description probably isn't accurate—honesty has its limits, as does self-knowledge. In this case, I am perched outside my own windows as I try to see into Carson's. Her house has been broken into, ransacked by looters. What am I looking for? What do they—the other biographers, critics, contemporaries—obscure from view?

Carson tried to preserve her history, including her inner life. After Mary's secretary, Barbara, transcribed the therapy tapes, Carson and Mary each got a copy to correct. When Carson was at Harkness Pavilion for one of several surgeries on her paralyzed left hand in the early 1960s, she pulled the transcript pages out of her hospital night table drawer and showed them to her agent, Robert Lantz. He took the stack home with him and found the material so memorable, he came to Mary looking for the pages after Carson's death. Lantz writes that he understood from Carson that the tapes were transcribed in order to develop a manuscript from which Carson might write a full autobiography. He insists to Mary that the pages he read "had vitality, directness, immense humor and of course are now of great historic value. They should certainly become part of the material to be made available to an approved biographer." Mary informed Lantz that the transcripts were Carson's "psychiatric records" and therefore strictly confidential.

To use her therapy transcripts as a source by which to construct Carson's autobiography is to accept a correlation between speaking and writing. It is not the same to speak as it is to write, but I have found my own writing increasingly inflected by, and arising as, something spoken, from a need to speak. For me, Carson's words are her words. I find it especially gratifying to hear her self-edit in the therapy sessions, changing the structure of a sentence, reframing a recollection, correcting and repeating herself so that all versions stand together on the page, a glut of words seeping forth without clear divisions, all in the interest of clarity.

*Illumination and Night Glare*, her published autobiography, was dictated to friends, nurses, secretaries, and students in

1967, during the last four months of her life. It picks up several of the threads of the therapy transcripts. But even when these pages were published in 1999, *Illumination and Night Glare* remained obviously unfinished, the scraps of her story. I imagine she was just getting started. Neither the therapy transcripts, which weren't made accessible until 2013, nor *Illumination* would figure largely in the biographies written about Carson, though they are the two surest examples of Carson telling her own version. While she was determined to write it, reciting her story from bed up to her last days, she never really had the chance. Who can tell the story of her own life?

# Unforeseen Events

I started to imagine that I had come to Columbus to convalesce, as Carson did throughout her twenties, neither my first nor my last delusion. Carson's bedridden state, her misdiagnoses, her various conditions that biographies make difficult to identify, gave me something tangible in common with her. She writes that in 1947, "finally, they discovered that I had a rheumatic heart condition as a child, and indeed too much running around put a strain on my heart so that it caused embolisms." While I stayed at Carson's, I struggled with my chronic illness, a heart condition that renders my body weak and constantly exhausted, prone to migraines and sudden sleep attacks, as I call them. It took months of testing for doctors to determine that my heart is too small, my blood volume too low, to keep my body afloat. My initial days in the house were slow: I fell asleep in the middle of my first morning and when I woke up it was nearly evening. I spent that week working my way back to feeling somewhat normal. Too weak to sit up, I took notes in my phone and tried to be present in the house. To feel what it was like to live there, and to figure out how I got there.

I hardly saw anyone while I was staying in Columbus, except a few students and professors at the brand-new university gym where I rowed every other day on the third floor, looking out on tall pines. One of the students working the front desk pretended she knew me so I could get a community membership for free: southern hospitality. And I got familiar with the librarians and local researchers hunting down their family trees at the university archive. The drive to campus along Hilton Avenue to Warm Springs Road threaded through mansions and old-growth trees, and it was what I saw most of in Columbus.

The Carson McCullers Center for Writers and Musicians held two events while I was in residence, and these were my only real social interactions all month. I rolled up my yoga mat and put away my sewing machine and tried to minimize my presence in the house. It wasn't clear to me whether or not it would be appropriate for me to hide out downstairs during these events, though that was my first inclination. My mind was a funny mix of Carson's biographies, which I was rereading diligently, and Super Tuesday election results and podcasts and Finnish lesbian cartoonist Tove Jansson's memoir, and I didn't quite know how I could surface from my cave and meet living people, let alone talk to them. But each time, at the last minute, I decided I should come up.

It seemed as though I ought to be answering the door, offering drinks, and taking coats, but everyone just waltzed right in. My first week they held a David Diamond memorial marimba concert—Diamond was Carson's friend, Reeves's lover—in the living room where Carson used to stage plays with her brother and sister. (Carson directed and starred.) For a few hours, the quiet house echoed with eerie plunks and was filled with strangers. No one talked to me. It had been days since I'd spoken face-to-face with anyone; I had trouble remembering how. The guests left as abruptly as they'd arrived, wheeling out their marimbas and reinstating my solitude without asking permission.

Later that month, I thought I would have better luck mingling at a student reading, with much of the English and writing department in attendance. But my main source of small talk was explaining why I was in the house. "I'm a writer," I offered. "I'm working on a book about McCullers." Using her last name seemed to make the enterprise more official, though I had yet to write a word about Carson. When I described the project and mentioned my interest in her relationships with women, I could have sworn multiple people backed away from me. Assuming I had made an odd impression but not sure why, I navigated the crowd into the back of the living room—my sewing room—and poured myself another glass of bad wine. Trying to use my body language as coded encouragement to the visitors to vacate the premises, I inched my way toward the door, where I landed on a new friend named Denis, who'd grown up Puerto Rican in Columbus. He didn't know much about Carson, but understood, he told me, what it meant to be an outsider in a town this conservative. He told me about the neighborhood, and how segregated Columbus remains, which my drives had indicated. Right off the bat he warned me that people here might not be thrilled to talk to me about my project, though he was, and we talked until everyone left. Denis explained that Columbus had its own understanding of Carson McCullers and what aspects of her life it was willing to recognize. Her sexuality, among other things, was not on the list.

I had arrived in Columbus thinking I might gain some context about Carson's material life, but I wasn't expecting to gain much insight into her personal life. I'd already rifled through the bulk of Carson's papers at the Ransom Center in Austin. The Columbus Public Library had asked Carson for her papers in 1961, and she replied that she would send them only if the library desegregated. They refused, and her papers went to Texas. That hasn't stopped the Columbus Library from retroactively celebrating her, naming the road that approaches their building Carson McCullers Way. During Carson's life, Columbus State University's archives, where the undestroyed portion of Mary's papers were donated after her death, did not yet exist. I visited these archives on an offhand tip from the director of the Carson McCullers Center, but I assumed that anything worth finding had already been written about. At that point, I knew of Mary as Carson's doctor and friend late in life. I'd come across photos of her at the Ransom Center when I scoured through all of Carson's personal albums, making a list of "possible girlfriends," but I hadn't considered Mary. I thought, if nothing else, thrilled as I am by diagnosis, the medical records Mary kept might be interesting.

On reading the therapy transcripts in the university's archive, I was so befuddled—with joy, excitement, fear—I could barely look at them long enough to process what they contained. I was stunned. Here was Carson, in person, trying to tell her story, to understand her sexuality, in her own words. And Mary, a willing listener. And, miracle of miracles, there it was, plain as day: the word "lesbian." I'm always reading queer histories that dance elaborately around the terminology of queerness, asserting that *at the time*, back then, people didn't describe themselves the way we do now. The effect of this, for me, is an erasure of lesbians from history. One of our many Foucauldian hangovers. But the word "lesbian" was like a magnet, pulling everything I had been researching to face it. I skimmed the messy, typed pages, I scanned them and emailed them to myself, and then, not knowing why, I put them away for months. I wasn't ready to deal with the Carson they contained, wasn't prepared to take her at her word.

Back at the house in the pink-and-yellow twilight, I called Chelsea and tried to explain to her the gravity of what I'd found. I walked in circles around the linoleum-floored kitchen, making curry soup with some previous resident's butternut squash I'd found on the windowsill, and paced back and forth across the pink carpeted rooms while it simmered. Chelsea didn't seem all that shocked. "Isn't that what you were looking for?" she asked. I stopped and glanced at the timeline of photographs on the dining room walls. Most of them are of Carson and Reeves, documenting their meeting, their courtship, their two marriages, before and after the war. I sat down on the living room floor. "Well, I didn't actually think I'd find it," I said.

# Becomings

Carson and Reeves moved to North Carolina, first Charlotte, then Fayetteville, soon after they married. Reeves later claimed that during that time he wrote a collection of essays, but no one saw his work. Reeves, a writer who never wrote, was credited by numerous critics and reviewers throughout Carson's life as the "real" Carson McCullers, the writer behind her books. There is no evidence to suggest even remotely that this might be the case. In Carson's words, "I must say that in all of his talk of wanting to be a writer, I never saw one single line he'd ever written except his letters."

Reeves was working as a credit salesman, though he rarely came home with any money, and Carson stayed in their shitty apartment all day, trying to write but unable to hear herself think over all the fighting next door. She describes her new marriage as "happy," but says that she was left alone in a house "divided into little rabbit warrens with plywood partitions, and only one toilet to serve ten or more people. In the room next door to me there was a sick child, an idiot, who bawled all day. The [husband] would come in and slap her, [and] the mother would cry." Carson was living in one of her own grotesque fictions. Carson and Reeves had never quite reached a level of comfort with physical intimacy. Reeves had cheated on her with one of her friends, Nancy, which he told her their first night together. Their new marriage was already starting to disintegrate. Carson went home, and Reeves stayed in North Carolina.

She returned to her parents' house in Columbus to begin a new book, "The Bride of My Brother," the original title for *The Member of the Wedding*. Shortly thereafter, in what would become a pattern of reversals for them, separating and reuniting, Carson and Reeves used the advance from her first book to move to New York. Reeves chose to sail first to Nantucket with his old roommate ("roommate"?), Jack Adams. Carson rode the bus by herself. She spent the publication day of *The Heart Is a Lonely Hunter*, June 14, 1940, in a boardinghouse room, "cut off and lonely." When the book appeared the reviews were staggering, especially for a twenty-three-year-old writer. They called her a child, baby-faced, and then in the same breath called her the new John Steinbeck. Richard Wright compared her to Faulkner, commending her "astonishing humanity that enables a white writer, for the first time in Southern fiction, to handle Negro characters with as much ease and justice as those of her own race." In an ad for the book in the *New York Times*, T. S. Stribling called it "the literary find of the year."

In the days following her book's publication, her own face in bookshop windows was the only friendly face in the city. That lonely summer, after paying a call to Greta Garbo, her idol, and finding her less than hospitable, and while waiting to hear back from Erika Mann, a lesbian transplant from Europe and daughter of novelist Thomas Mann, Carson received a telegram from her editor, Robert Linscott, to meet at the Bedford Hotel. Carson writes that she went right out and bought a new summer suit, wanting badly to look the part of celebrated young writer and unable to do so in her cotton sundresses schlepped from Georgia. At the Bedford, Carson recalls, "a stranger" arrived. "She had a face that I knew would haunt me to the end of my life," she writes in *Illumination*, "beautiful, blonde, with straight short hair. She asked me to call her [Annemarie] right away, and we became friends immediately. At her invitation, I saw her the next day."

Annemarie Clarac-Schwarzenbach was one of the many lesbians Carson encountered in her new life in New York, and she was among the most glamorous. She wore custom suits from Paris, her hair was chicly cropped, and her features severe and gorgeous. Or, as female writer R. L. York puts it, "Her head was a Donatello David head; her blonde hair was smooth and cut like a boy's; her blue eyes dark and slow moving; her mouth childish and soft with shyly parted lips. She wore a skirt and boy's shirt and a blue blazer and she was not afraid of my dog." When Carson and Annemarie met again the following day, they talked about Annemarie's morphine addiction (Carson had never heard of the drug) and her travels in Afghanistan, Egypt, Syria, and the Far East.

Carson immediately fell hard for Annemarie. Who wouldn't? She'd been dreaming of escaping Columbus and the South for years, and with her first book she had finally gotten out. The arrival of Annemarie offered her something else that she had been longing for without the language to express it. Annemarie told Carson that when she was seventeen, her mother had called her "a dope fiend, a communist, and a lesbian," which was how she wound up in New York. Annemarie tried to remain polite to her mother, though she had little feeling for her. But when she would go home to Switzerland, York says, "she would don her most feminine blouse, pull her stockings straight, and set out to go visiting." After she was gone, the neighbors would say, "'Really a lovely girl, if it were not for the awful things one hears about her,'" York writes. "That was generally the epitaph." Little remains of Carson's interactions with Annemarie, but it's clear from her letters and from the therapy transcripts that Carson was not shy about her feelings at the time or afterward. She did not disguise them or even question them. She loved Annemarie, and that was that.

Before I left for the house in Georgia, I spent several afternoons looking at over a thousand photos from Carson's collection at the Ransom Center. Is it perhaps too intimate to keep using her first name? I no longer worked there, but Chelsea did, and she saw that a scholar had pulled all these boxes, so she told me to come in. The other scholar was doing some kind of project about tomboys. Carson really wasn't a tomboy, whatever that is, as far as I can tell. I cannot imagine her displaying athletic ability, and she was by no means butch. The possessiveness I feel: *I know her better.* This feeling of kinship is common with beloved authors, Carson in particular. After visiting Columbus, novelist Elizabeth McCracken writes of Carson, "I begin to believe that if only I had a chance to talk to her . . . surely, at any time, if we'd met we'd become good friends. . . . I'd tell her she was better than that old Nunnally Johnson, that terrible Gore Vidal. We would've understood each other." The illusion: feeling understood *by* someone does not equate to understanding them. But the illusion is powerful, convincing. It is rare to recognize when you are under its sway.

I came across a series of photos of Annemarie in Carson's files. It seems Carson may have taken them when they were out on a walk one day, but where and when I can't tell. It is possible that she collected them, and I can't blame her. The day is sunny. Annemarie is striking, deeply androgynous yet somehow femme, something about the delicacy of her features. Today she would be a model. Céline would put her in an oversized boyfriend shirt and sell millions. This is the woman who shaped Carson's entire idea of love, prior to Mary. In the photos she leans on a fence, crouches on a sidewalk, dares the camera. While I sifted through the photos and tried to understand where they came from, I could see Chelsea in a room just to my left, in a meeting. We'd been having a tense day over text, miscommunicating about plans, but when I walked in prepared to be somewhat irritated with her, there she was looking lovely, her long dark hair, her posture, and she smiled. And then waved. I love her.

After Reeves arrived in the city, he hung around their fifth floor Greenwich Village apartment all day, leaving only to go to the bars. Carson recalls staying out late one night with Annemarie and when she came home she found Reeves "worried and furious with me." He asked her what they had been doing "all night."

"Just talking," she said.

"Are you in love with Mademoiselle Schwarzenbach?" (That "mademoiselle" sounds so condescending to me.)

"I don't know," she said. At that, he slapped her, then slapped her again, "quick and powerful as a panther." In *Illumination*, Carson writes, "later, I begged Reeves to try to get a job so he wouldn't be hanging around the apartment all day wasting time. The apartment, by the way, was on West 11th Street near the docks." Carson's "by the way" was likely code for saying she knew Reeves was spending his time with sailors down at the docks, pursuing men, possibly women. She concludes, "the utter uselessness of his life depressed me, and that complete moral depression lasted until his death. I was writing all the time which must [have gotten on] his nerves. I really don't know how I stood those months," referring to the months when they lived together.

# February House

Carson got away from Reeves and their New York apartment long enough to attend her first literary retreat, the Bread Loaf Writer's Conference, in Middlebury, VT, in August 1940. She met Eudora Welty and Louis Untermeyer, in whom she found models for how she might occupy her new role as writer. She liked being with other writers; she felt at home with them. She began to imagine a different life for herself. When she came back to New York, she went into the *Harper's Bazaar* offices every day to work with editor George Davis on *Reflections in a Golden Eye,* her second book, which they were publishing serially that fall. One day, he told Carson, "[since] you don't get along with Reeves and live in such a miserable apartment, why don't you live with me?" They decided that the answer to both their problems—her stifling marriage, his stifling budget—was to find a house where they could live and work together, with other writers and artists who were similarly inclined. George Davis was an openly gay man, but Carson still made sure that he meant for them to live together "as brother and sister." "My prudery came through," she wrote in *Illumination*. When they found a house in Brooklyn at 7 Middagh Street, Carson moved out of the apartment with Reeves. Reeves was allowed to come over for dinner, but he could not stay the night.

Soon enough the house was filled with queers: British poet Wystan (W. H.) Auden, whom Carson unfailingly called Winston; composer couple Peter Pears and Benjamin Britten; writer couple Christopher Isherwood and Louis MacNeice. And, in time, renowned cabaret performer and struggling writer Gypsy Rose Lee, and Paul and Jane Bowles, a married couple who were both queer—a complicated, though common enough, marriage of convenience. Carson writes, "everyone had their own room and there was a large parlor and a big dining room, and Gypsy Rose Lee . . . found us a cook. Everyone went out of his way to give us gifts, as though we were some kind of a multiple bridal party." Friends came to visit, including Annemarie, Erika Mann and her girlfriends, and lesbian power couple Janet Flanner and Solita Solano. Janet would become one of Carson's "many-gendered mothers" (Dana Ward by way of Maggie Nelson) in the queer community, making introductions for her in New York and later in Europe.

Queerness wasn't closeted at February House, so-named by writer Anaïs Nin because most of the residents were born in February. An Aquarius myself, I can see the appeal of living under one roof, but in separate bedrooms, with a troupe of fellow Aquarians: eccentric, creative, and independent creatures. Acceptance of others' lives and relationships was a precondition for being invited over, and for several years it was a place to which many New York writers and artists longed to be invited. Reeves, deeply homophobic and in the midst of a lifelong struggle with his own sexuality, wasn't fond of all the queer goings on at February House, especially in close proximity to Carson.

But Carson was finally at home. "At last, after all the years of apartment misery I was living in a comfortable, even luxurious house. My room was of Empire green, very simple and with a small dressing room adjoining. We all paid our share of the expenses, so the house was not too costly." They threw parties—"I had the most wonderful sawdust parties in the world," Carson tells Mary—which might refer to parties while the Middagh Street house was in the midst of renovations, or parties for which guests paid a fee or brought gifts. They were also trying to establish a steady working schedule for the house, but after-hours, Carson and George went regularly to the bars of Sands Street and to the cabarets. Brooklyn was full of sailors, to George's delight, and in the war years, at least among certain circles, queer desire and behaviors were recognized and celebrated.

# Imaginary Friends

At February House, Carson pined over Annemarie to Gypsy, who comforted her and told her she wasn't worth her time. Apparently, everyone told Carson this. Annemarie was in a long, tortured relationship with the married Baroness Margot von Opel, not to mention a long, tortured relationship with morphine, not to mention she was still in love with Erika Mann. Many friends warned Carson against getting involved with her.

Though they aren't easy to follow, the therapy transcripts allow Carson to speak loudly and clearly for herself, and a large portion of them focus on her relationship with Annemarie. The first recorded session begins with the words "I've been thinking of Annamarie S." At first I thought "Annamarie" might be typo on the part of the transcriber, Barbara, or a phonetic reflection of the way Carson said her name, lilting and southern. But throughout *Illumination*, she writes her name as Anna Marie. How we make beloved others our own.

Carson was back in Georgia in November 1940, recovering from illness and taking a break from February House, when she heard that Annemarie had attempted suicide. After escaping Blithe View, the psychiatric institution where she'd been placed, Annemarie sent a telegram asking Carson to come see her at the mutual friend's apartment where she was staying. Carson immediately boarded a night train for New York. When Carson arrived at the apartment, Annemarie was playing Mozart endlessly on the gramophone. She was delirious and desperate for morphine, and at first she didn't even recognize Carson. Instead she started asking her for Dr. February, a woman Annemarie claimed gave her insulin shock treatments and then "made love" to her while she was institutionalized. She tells Mary she couldn't believe Annemarie was asking for Dr. February after she had travelled so far to be with her. Carson was, naively but earnestly, expecting a warmer, more heartfelt welcome. Annemarie began asking Carson to get her some dope, so Carson took matters into her own hands and walked down the street to a bar. Carrying a martini in each hand several blocks back to Annemarie, she thought, *Here goes the night.* The transcript shifts abruptly back to Carson dictating a letter to Sir Carrol Reed about producing a film version of *Reflections in a Golden Eye*, but Carson revisits this one night with Annemarie in each subsequent session.

At their appointment four days later, Mary and Carson begin with a conversation about different types of love.

Carson tells Mary that reciprocity in love does exist, but
is extremely unlikely, because of the faith in another person it demands. She doesn't finish the sentence, unable or
unwilling to put into words what the effect of unrequited
love might be in the abstract. Unrequited love, feelings
unreturned, was a fear that haunted Carson. In these first
few sessions, she describes her own experience with love as
a series of triangulated pursuits and doomed missed connections. Biographers have used the triangulated or unful-
filled love stories in her novels (Frankie and her brother's
wedding, the private, the officer, and the wife in *Reflections*,
Singer and Antonapoulos, Amelia and Cousin Lymon) to
argue that Carson didn't believe two people could love
each other, that she never experienced true shared love,
but only loved those who did not love her back, or failed
to love those who loved her deeply. This, conveniently,
makes it easy for biographers to dismiss Carson's own professions of love for Annemarie and other women—they
belie, just like all of her characters', impossible longings.

And perhaps categorizing her own feelings as unrequited
love was a way for Carson to avoid fully recognizing the
implications of her longings, or what it would mean to
carry them out. I can affirm that a reverse of this strategy
was useful in my own life, and I imagine it is a common
practice for many closeted queers, whose identities are unacknowledged even to themselves. We figure ourselves out
via these longings, lustings, envies. Perhaps the fantasy of

a crush leaves room for imagination, a space that makes crushes so luscious, so self-sustaining in their way. Without pursuing them, they can be so much more, can be anything we want them to be. They never have a chance to disappoint. Throughout adolescence and high school, even as I was heading into college, I constructed straight crushes and love interests as a sort of defense mechanism against ever pursuing a relationship or considering one seriously. I would develop a hopeless crush on some guy who I barely knew, or was older than I was, and when I sat up at night on the phone with friends who inevitably wanted to talk about guys, I always had someone to talk about. At the time, of course, I thought I was in love. I didn't know it was a form of evasion. But it occurred to me years later that this was a convenient way to avoid ever actually dating anyone, or thinking seriously about my feelings. I didn't realize I had feelings for another woman until my first girlfriend in college pursued me, and I had to come to terms with what I felt. It's possible that, without her, I never would have allowed myself to desire anyone with awareness and serious intent. It takes the right circumstances, the right person for our own desires to out us to ourselves.

Perhaps Carson's pining for impossible or unrelenting love interests throughout her life reflects a similar strategy, unconscious though it may have been. Carson called the other women she loved her "imaginary friends" with Reeves, and clearly their existence caused Reeves to feel insecure even when he and Carson weren't married or officially together. Yet by calling them imaginary, it seems like Carson is trying to dismiss or downplay her own feelings. Were these friends imaginary because Carson did not pursue them romantically? Or imaginary because Carson only daydreamed about them, without taking action? Imaginary because somehow having feelings for them was not as real as having feelings for someone else? Savigneau writes that "imaginary friends" was a phrase both Carson and Reeves used to refer to "Carson's passions. All too often they totally took over her life and her mind for several weeks or several months during which Carson used what she called her 'beloved' as an excuse to refuse somewhat more peremptorily to let Reeves come close or touch her." An excuse. A buffer. An evasion. A way of protecting herself to assert herself/control the narrative.

Mary tells her, "I do believe that there is such a thing as mature love but it takes devotion and discipline on both people's part. People are so starved for love, so greedy, that at the first sign of emotional attraction and response, their tendency is to clutch and wish to merge and in the end the hope for love escapes them. It takes a great deal of courtesy and ability to see and love the difference, the separateness of the other. To be willing to let the other person be himself, [sic] free, different." I can't help but flag the use of "himself" here, the presumption that love exists between an "I" and a "he," despite Carson's focus on Annemarie. But Mary offers Carson the idea of a love that respects the other, which she had never experienced herself. In a fashion that will become characteristic of their letters, Mary brings in a poet to help explain: "Rilke's definition of mature love concerns this," she says, "that two solitudes protect, border and salute each other. It is the difference between falling in love and standing in love."

Knowing that their relationship will blossom into love during and following these months of therapy together, it is hard not to read these lines as a suggestion, as Mary opening up the possibility of love to Carson in more than just a theoretical way. I am especially struck by the emotional openness of Mary's words to Carson in the transcripts, as so often on paper—in her letters to Carson's lawyers and biographers—she comes off cold. Closed off. *Destroy them.* Perhaps this is the effect of reading only the history that exists in writing. Without the transcripts, their voices, their spoken rhythms are lost. I know so little about Mary, about who she was.

Carson responds by returning to the subject of Annemarie. Mary asks her why she and Annemarie had never slept together, the million-dollar question, and Carson insists at first that because Annemarie was so drugged out, she couldn't possibly have made love to her. She loved her, respected her too much. But the passage ends with the beginning of a sentence suggesting that perhaps she may have.

The page ends there.

# Prove It on Me Blues

Of course, this is killing me. The gaps in the transcript, the messiness of it all. I've been trying to find out if Carson and Annemarie did it for years now. When their relationship is acknowledged at all, it is usually given a disparaging account that is short on detail.

On the next page of the transcript, a handwritten addition to the typed version at the top of the page finishes the sentence, that yes, she could have made love to her.

Several lines of blank space follow, and then, typed in all caps, separated by empty lines that may or may not indicate erasures (did Barbara erase as she transcribed? Was it hard to hear what Carson was saying? Are these just protracted pauses?), a fragment that reads like Sappho. She did sleep with Annemarie, though still she felt distanced from her, that they both sensed it.

I put the pages down with an audible, exasperated sigh and suddenly came back into the small Columbus reading room.

For the first time in hours I looked up from my round table covered in stacks of folders at the other researchers—pairs of sisters or cousins all trying to find out their genealogical histories—and I began to question my research impulses. I'd found the love letters four years ago. I recognized what I read. What more proof did I think I needed? What was I trying to prove? Historians demand proof from queer love stories that they never require of straight relationships. Unless someone was in the room when the two women had sex (and just what "sex" means between women is, for many historians, up for debate), there's just no reason to include in the historical record that they were lesbians. At least that's what it seems like to me.

Part of this is a hangover from the romantic friendship, a well-documented and socially sanctioned kind of relationship between women in the eighteenth and nineteenth centuries that bore all the trappings of romantic love—shared homes, finances, love letters—except sex, which was generally unacknowledged in all types of relationships. Whether or not we are aware of it, this prudish, Victorian version of women loving women shapes what we believe such relationships mean. The demand for proof itself became a useful way for women to hide the sexual nature of their relationships in the early twentieth century, as it had been in prior decades. They were innocent—straight—until proven guilty. Ma Rainey, a black singer-songwriter and the (lesbian) mother of the blues, incidentally also born in Columbus, Georgia, records this maneuver exquisitely in her song called "Prove It on Me Blues:" "Went out last night with a crowd of my friends / They must've been women, 'cause I don't like no men. . . . They say I do it, ain't nobody caught me / They sure got to prove it on me."

In the UK, when lawmakers were revising the laws that criminalized gay sex to further discourage homosexual behavior, it was determined best not to outlaw sex between women. This is not because it was condoned, but because lawmakers—men—believed that if sex between women was so much as mentioned in the law, it would alert women to the possibility and encourage women to have sex with each other. Best to keep as many in the dark as possible. And so sex between women remained in most places legal and unspoken. Feminist author Stella Browne wrote in 1915, "the realities of women's sexual life have been greatly obscured by the lack of any sexual vocabulary . . . the conventionally 'decently brought up girl,' of the upper and middle classes, has no terms to define many of her sensations and experiences." Certainly this dearth of language applies to Carson.

Carson continues her account of that night with Annemarie in the words she has available. As Carson handed her the martini, a meager substitute for morphine, Annemarie threw a fit of jealousy over Margot von Opel, her married ex who had recently taken out a restraining order on her. Annemarie demanded that Carson call Margot at her house in Florida.

Margot did not want to talk. Shifting gears, Annemarie ordered Carson to remove what she was wearing, and then she began to touch her. A blank in the manuscript follows, perhaps a long silence while Carson finds the precise, unfortunate words to describe what appears to be her first sexual encounter with a woman—if only I could share them with you. She was certain she had Annemarie at last, and she describes all of her systems—fluids—firing at once—she cried, she sweat, she got wet, though she isn't sure how to say that. The ellipses in the transcript seem to indicate pauses, rather than missing words. Suddenly, juices flowing, Annemarie told Carson she was too skinny, she wanted Gypsy Rose Lee, Carson's housemate, instead. According to Annemarie, people had seen Carson and Gypsy together at night clubs, and she knew that they had stayed together over weekends. She demanded that Carson fetch Gypsy for her, and offered to let her watch while they fucked. Carson fled the room naked. This moment of stark humiliation likely defined Carson's understanding of love, of sex, of intimacy between women for many years.

Moments later, Annemarie had locked herself in the bathroom, "cutting her wrists and trying to cut her throat." The police showed up. At some point, Carson tells Mary, Carson picked up a chair and told the police that her grandfather had been an Irish cop like them, which was a lie, and that she refused to allow them to arrest Annemarie without calling a doctor. Annemarie's doctor was called. Mary tells

Carson, "everything you have said lent sanity to an insane situation. . . . You had to act under that much pressure. You could act. This is heroism." On her way out of the apartment, Carson recalls in therapy, Annemarie came after her to ask for her forgiveness and to tell her she loved her. In *Illumination*, Carson notes only that as she left the apartment, Annemarie said "Thank you, my liebling," and kissed her. "It was the first and last time we ever kissed each other," Carson writes. She makes no mention in print of their other interactions that night, prompting Savigneau to write in her biography, "how likely are two lovers who never shared a passionate kiss?"

# Dedications

Shortly after that night, Annemarie was given the option of being institutionalized or leaving the country, and she moved abroad. Carson dedicated her second book, *Reflections in a Golden Eye*, "For Annemarie Clarac-Schwarzenbach." Like *Heart*, the novel takes up hidden queer desire between men, this time on an army base. However, perhaps because the desire is more explicitly sexual in *Reflections*, or perhaps because it takes place on an army base that looks a lot like nearby Fort Benning, the book was not well received by her friends and neighbors back home in Georgia. In *Reflections*, a young private is obsessed with watching the wife of a captain sleep through the window of her house at night. The captain, meanwhile, lusts after the private without quite understanding his own interest. Carson's inspiration came from a Peeping Tom incident at a nearby army base that Reeves had told her about years before. Contending with her angry neighbors in conservative Columbus, who apparently recognized too much of themselves in her (to them) salacious fiction, Carson teased, "everybody accused me of writing about everybody else, so that I must say I didn't realize the morals of the [Army] post were that corrupt."

Home for a visit in the winter of 1941 after the book came out, Carson got a phone call from a member of the local KKK who threatened her life, telling her she wouldn't be allowed to survive the night after publishing a book like *Reflections*. "We don't like n—lovers or fairies," they informed her, likely referring to her focus on black characters in *Heart* and on gay desire in *Reflections*. Carson's father, Lamar, brought a policeman to the house to protect her. That same night, Carson came down with what they thought was pneumonia and spent several days unconscious. When she awoke, she had no recollection of the call and couldn't understand the numbers on the clock to tell what time it was. Though no one knew it then, this was her first stroke. Her sight returned, but she was unable to walk for a month.

By the fall of 1941, Carson had divorced Reeves. She had spent her first summer in residence at Yaddo, where she began a new work that would be called *Ballad of the Sad Café*. When she returned to New York, she learned from her father that over the summer, Reeves had forged her signature on the check she received from *The New Yorker* for her short story "The Jockey," and had done the same with several of her royalties checks. Carson writes, "it was clear that Reeves was a very sick man and needed more help than I could give him. When I faced him with this accusation, he denied it completely and imperturbably. I went to a lawyer and told him the story, and we were divorced at City Hall almost immediately." Reeves had been living with David Diamond while Carson was away. By all appearances Reeves and David had been sleeping together.

After her split from Reeves, and after that night with Annemarie, Carson fell ill. She was alone in New York and couldn't see properly. Bouts of temporary blindness were an effect of her stroke. She couldn't make out the place to sign on a check and had to call her friend Muriel Rukeyser, a poet, for help. At that point, she again returned to Columbus to regain her strength and recuperate. Much to her surprise, Annemarie began to write to her, to apologize and explain what happened back in New York. While Annemarie seemed so heartless that night, what she calls "the last bad time," reading these letters reveals shades of her love and devotion to Carson. As Carson saw, there was more to Annemarie than the suicidal addict, the cold seductress. In her own way, at a distance, she loved Carson back.

*Thysville, December 29th, 1941 Belgian Congo. . . . You don't know, Carson, how happy your letter made me. . . . Further, I never regret anything, not even my experiences of the last bad time in N.Y., nor now the war experience of Africa, because we live in a world, and we only get to feel and live and write down the deeper sense, and the deepest agony, love, and [fraud? illegible] of our life by confronting it in an eternal struggle with the world-partner. . . . Carson, I can talk so easily to you, about things which really are the subject of my book: I think it deals with our own nun heritage, our relation to men, to what we call friend and enemy, our bitter loving fight with the world first, then with the angel who leads us back to the reborn calm of death and eternity. . . . In sad and lonely hours, I think of how close and with how infinite tenderness you and I would understand each other.*

# Ambivalences

Annemarie's letters were a great comfort to Carson, helping her recover from her divorce and her frightening illness and find her way back into *Member of the Wedding*. But during these months, Carson spent many days and nights in her old bedroom in Columbus crying over Annemarie's departure. When her sister Rita came home for a visit, she decided to out Carson to her parents. Rita was fifteen and just back from her first year of college. Carson was twenty and had had her heart broken by a woman.

I knew I didn't like Rita from a distance. In all the photos of the two of them, they look like sisters, which they are, but they look that way because their faces say so. They say maybe Rita can't stand Carson and never could. Carson's big eyes look straight into the camera or into her sister's eyes if she faces her, but Rita cuts her eyes and looks away. Rita called both their parents into their shared bedroom and informed them that Carson was a lesbian. Everyone in the family called Carson "Sister." Carson recalls that her dad responded to Rita by asking her what that was—as though he'd never heard the term "lesbian." Rita explained that Carson had fallen in love with a woman, and therefore she couldn't stand to stay in the same room as her. A moment of exposure, a possible recognition of Carson's lesbian experience, was swiftly negated by her father, who told Rita that Sister was a beautiful and wonderful daughter and that Rita should aspire to be even half as wonderful as she. (His response gives a possible explanation for some of Rita's palpable resentment of her older sister.)

When I brought my first girlfriend home over the summer after my freshman year of college, home to my version of Columbus, a north-shore Chicago suburb, a WASP paradise, we were officially roommates. We—me, my "roommate," and my parents—were sitting at the table after dinner, when my staunchly Catholic mom took the opportunity to read aloud to us from my notebooks that I had left behind over break, which she found in my room while I was away at school. All through childhood and adolescence at home, my mom had regularly rifled through my drawers, my closet. It was her house, she insisted; she had the right. My first year at college, I regularly filled and discarded notebooks, though after this incident I stopped writing for several years. Perhaps on some level I knew that by leaving them behind, she'd read them. My mom was infuriated. She made a spectacle of reading aloud about a relationship that we had barely admitted to each other, she read aloud "baby" and "love."

My girlfriend fled to the basement. It was nothing, I insisted to my parents. She could prove nothing. We were friends. I pressed hard on the ambiguity of my words, my handwriting, and refused to admit who or what I had written about. Instinctively I denied everything.

Enraged, exposed, I fled the house with my love, to the Chicago Botanic Garden for a walk. There's nowhere to go in the suburbs. As we circled the familiar paths, she said to me, "You know, she's right. We should stop this." Stop lying? I wondered. No. What she meant was we should stop being together, end our relationship, go back to being friends. My world shattered. "You aren't real," I heard. "You don't matter. This love doesn't count."

These exposures and their swift negations—one moment outed, the next told by my girlfriend that what I thought was love was to her a bad habit we ought to break—are just some of the bait-and-switch effects of closeting and denial. To be outed is a violation, but it is also a moment of freedom, of honesty, of finally being out of hiding. When what is real is never fully public, it ceases in effect to be real. I thought it was a problem with narrative, with story, with word choice, but suddenly I saw it as a breakdown in ontology. In being and its meaning. The language used to describe reality defines and determines that reality, more than I ever knew. Beneath my feet the meaning of our relationship shifted, and my ability to know my own identity slid away with it. If this wasn't love, what was it? Who was I? And why couldn't I speak up for it, call it by name? There was such loss and confusion in this rejection for me, in a relationship where any miscommunication could have been a denial of what I thought was real. Everything was so freighted. The world shattered at that moment, for if this was nothing, the fear became: will I ever have it again? If I'm back in the closet, how will I ever be anything but alone? Relying on one person to define what is possible is a product of relationships borne in secrecy. It's also a reason to hang on to that relationship, no matter how painful it is. The denials of our love as public fact continued for six more years. I hung on for something. I waited. I moved to Austin with her, we set up our first apartment together. Again, we were roommates. We didn't tell any of our old or new friends the truth. Because if we couldn't name it to ourselves, what would we have said?

Soon enough Carson was open with her mother, Bebe, about her relationships with Annemarie and with Reeves. (Bebe had met both Annemarie and Gypsy while visiting Carson at February House. She "loved Gypsy, but she didn't care for Annamarie.") According to Virginia Carr, Bebe "knew of Carson's ambivalences and accepted them un-questioningly," though her father was never fully informed. Presumably he would not have understood. Ambivalence, as far as I can tell, is a highly coded way for Carson's first major biographer to communicate "lesbian" or "queer" or "not straight" desire. Ambivalence, which could just as easily suggest confusion, indecision. A woman who doesn't know her own mind, her own wants.

# Convalescence

Again and again Carson retreated to Columbus, to the South, to her mother, to her old house to convalesce and to write. Carson wrote in the morning and the afternoon, and then took her bath before dinner, but in her house I took baths just about all day. I could read there and write there and spend long stretches alone with my body, and the ceiling, and the medicinal smell of mustard bath. My aching head, my weak legs could finally relax underwater, in an all-pink bathroom at the front of the house with a sign that says Public Restroom that I chose to ignore. The other bathrooms were all blue and all teal, respectively, and the one downstairs had peeling wallpaper with ducks on it—I just couldn't be in there. I don't think I was meant to use that tub, I don't think anyone was, but the bathroom was big and bright and airy, across the hall from what used to be Carson's bedroom, and I felt at home there.

When she was home, she stayed in the childhood bedroom she had shared with Rita, and where I sat at the marble table from Carson's house in Nyack, New York, that now takes up the entire room. The room is at the front of the house and its windows look out on magnolias and rose-bushes. This is the room where I feel Carson's presence most strongly, but I think that might be because her belongings—her suitcase, her wristwatch, a single worn white glove—line the walls in glass cases. It is shrine-like, and only once, at the end of my stay, did I venture in there after dark. The room's closets have been converted into vitrines with glass windows for doors. Some of the objects they contain are things she held and used regularly. Her panto eyeglasses, her typewriter, a portable record player. A lighter, a cigarette case, an ice bucket. How these items conjure a lifestyle, a person's body in motion. Carson lighting a cigarette, playing a record, filling her glass with ice. It's her childhood bedroom, but no mementos from childhood remain. Instead, a metal shoehorn. A trunk. A key on a key ring, a checkbook, a wallet, a purse. All signal the adult Carson, from when she still went out regularly, still traveled and looked after herself. Symbols of the times when she was free and unconfined by infirmity. There's a framed Cecil Beaton photo that Chelsea, when she came to pick me up at the end of the month, was horrified to see sitting out in the changing sunlight all day. And there I was pouring steam out under the bathroom door, making everything worse. But Georgia is basically a swamp, so it seemed to me it was only a matter of time before everything warped, curled, lost its crispness. I imagine the

91

stationery sets in the cases have felt damp to the touch for years. Outside the windows that early spring, the Japanese magnolias were in bloom.

*On the boat, from Portuguese Angola to Lisbon. March 20th, 1942.*
*My dear, dear little Carson,*
*. . . if I didn't write to you at once, Carson, my darling, I was deeply shaken by your letter. I do know that your illness is but the counterpart of your sensibility and talent, and I know that suffering and solitude burns our ego, burns all selfish weakness, frees us, and will deeply help your work. But to write, you need a certain strength. Oh Carson, be patient, you must get slowly well again! Believe me, even if you feel shaken and can't write for a long time, this doesn't matter: you will express what God wants you to express, and be what he meant you to be: we cannot judge the results (as, finally, we can't and should not judge the effects of what we write), but we must give our greatest effort. Be patient. Don't say that we will not meet again. This is also a more hazardous question, but I live with the intense wish of love and friendship towards you, the feeling that you live, and love me, and that you write in the same absolute spirit, and that your books might be better or purer than mine could be—this is a hope and consolation for me. Darling, let us be ready to meet each other, whenever it will be possible. And*

*do, as you wrote, do everything to get well . . . The one*
*I love is you as if you were my sister. I kiss you. Your*
*Annemarie.*

In letters like these, she's giving Carson the support and
motivation that she needs to keep writing through physical weakness, paralysis, and pain, but it's hard not to see
the moments where Annemarie belittles, condescends, or
snatches the love she seems to offer back at the last moment. York writes that when Annemarie met other writers,
"she had long talks with them, and let them fall in love
with her or use her as a theme." When I narrated Carson's
relationship with Annemarie to Chelsea for the thousandth
time, trying to parse that "sister" in the letter's last line, she
replied, "God, Annemarie is such a type."

# Parasites

Early on in my stay at Carson's house, I woke in the middle of the night certain that I had a parasite, or many tiny ones, because of the way something moved in my stomach. I didn't let myself Google it in the night—the Wi-Fi signal was weak in my cave—just eventually fell back to sleep. The next morning, I read that exhaustion is one of the symptoms of intestinal parasites, as are anxiety and waking up in the night. Now I was scared to eat because I might feed them. I was still adjusting to the reality of my diagnosis, the reality that I would almost always feel weak, tired, slow. I spent a lot of time researching other possible explanations for my symptoms, acute conditions that could be cured expediently. It felt better to me to imagine a parasite than to accept that this sloth-like creature was just who I was. Only later did it occur to me that I might very well be feeling possessed in other ways.

# Homebodies

I came to feel that I was part of the house, its rhythms, its long life. In the kitchen I found the oldest stand mixer in the world, a ten-speed Dormeyer, and made cardamom shortbread, blueberry pie. I ate breakfast at the table in the wallpapered dining room off the kitchen, knowing all the while that this was the room from which Carson drew for *Member of the Wedding*; this was the kitchen where so much of the book takes place, Frankie and Berenice and John Henry sitting across from me rolling out biscuit dough. The house and I carried on a conversation, even if it didn't always answer my questions. I think back to a Q and A I once attended with Ruth Franklin, the biographer of midcentury writer Shirley Jackson, in North Bennington, VT, Jackson's hometown. "She built houses in her fiction," one questioner declared. "Please tell us which of her houses these were."

Slowly I settled in, though there were things about living in a museum that were not totally comfortable or clear. I kept taking long, migraineous naps on the couch where the director told me Carson wrote *Clock Without Hands*, a mod white sofa that is allegedly grimy—I didn't remove the slip-cover to see. The couch appears in a photo of Carson taken by Cecil Beaton. She's stretched out in her embroidered vest holding her cane. I didn't even know if I was supposed to sit on it—or on any of the furniture—but there really wasn't anywhere else to sit. Yet only a few years prior, working in an archive, I handled the belongings of writers, Carson included, wearing white gloves and tissue paper. I got a quilt from the closet—hers? I hoped not—and within a week I was sleeping and eating dinner and watching movies on the couch. I watched *Who's Afraid of Virginia Woolf?* and other burned DVDs Chelsea sent me in the mail from her collection, annotated with Post-it notes: "Classic—academic horrorshow—brilliant—60s." The movie made me feel a little glum about relationships; the two are so horrible to each other, and I kept thinking about Carson and Reeves. I rented *Reflections in a Golden Eye*, the movie made of Carson's second novel right before she died, and laughed out loud at the absurd last shot. The camera flashes back and forth from one character to another after Elizabeth Taylor's gay husband shoots the private he's been obsessed with throughout the film—the private who, meanwhile, had been sneaking into his bedroom to watch his wife sleep.

# Rules

No one told me not to sit on the furniture. No one told me not to set up my sewing machine and lay out my chambray fabric on the living room table, scattering the carpet with dark blue threads. I would pick them up eventually. No one told me not to play the classical CD that was already in the boom box; certainly no one told me not to dance. No one told me not to unroll my yoga mat in the foyer and practice across from the huge, bad portrait of Carson over the mantel. No one told me not to sit on my kneeling desk chair I brought with me from home at the marble table where Carson lunched with her idol, Isak Dinesen, and Marilyn Monroe. No one told me not to open the drawers or find Carson's high school yearbook. Beside her black-and-white photo, it reads Carson Smith, "Music, when soft voices die, vibrates in the memory." Carson's hair is slicked back and tucked behind her ears. Someone has curled the bottom under. She wears a dark jacket with a rumpled white lapel folded over it. She looks far away.

# My Rainbow Youth

I came to Carson first through her love letters, and then through her clothes. As an intern at the Ransom Center, a vault of books and manuscripts, I was given a choice of second-year projects. Anything I wanted to work on, any collection that needed cataloging, any exhibition in the works could have been my focus. After a year of detouring to push my library cart down aisles of typewriters, eyeglasses, and—most amazingly—clothes every time I was on the seventh floor, I knew that I wanted to work on the personal effects collections. I was assigned the clothing, objects, and miscellaneous housewares of four writers: Gertrude Stein, Alice B. Toklas, Sir Arthur Conan Doyle, and Carson McCullers. Before this project, I hadn't thought all that much about an author's clothes. But in my hours with random assortments of garments—socks, suits, coats, hats, and vests—I became more convinced of their potential for communing with lives past.

Since I'd unearthed Annemarie's letters and realized how insignificantly she came off in Carson's public story, I began to cling to Carson's mentions of places and objects for clues to who she was. Her clothes, her knickknacks, offered something I came to see as more truthful: the honesty of objects. Description can only expose so much of the self or contain so much of a memory or an experience. Photos and objects offer alternative access points to Carson's history of identity formation and love. When I first reached for these objects, trying to understand Carson's story, I was reaching for an embodied history, a past I could touch.

Carson's focus on clothes in her therapy sessions and in *Illumination* reveals their importance to her, which I intuited while I catalogued them. Clothes gave her a way to express an identity that was fluid, a way to change who she was to the world each day. In April 1958, Carson laments to Mary her long lost status as an "it girl," wistful for her former stylishness. In her more elegant days, she wore what she called *costumes* made by a friend, Joyce Davis, and her girlfriends were the most attractive around. At bars like the Blue Angel, the 21 Club, and Alice's Candle, they gallivanted in box-pleated skirts and knee-high socks and peacoats. Named for the 1930 Marlene Dietrich film, the Blue Angel was a cabaret in Manhattan where Barbra Streisand would later perform. Carson mentions someone by the name of Crawford, but the first name is blank. *Joan?* I marvel. In her years in New York, when she lived on and off at February House, Carson spent her time with queer writers and tastemakers in bars and cabarets all over town.

This joyful memory is undercut by "Annamarie and her agony, you know, and Gypsy, and Annette." The drama of her twenties.

When I catalogued Carson's clothes, I took them off the hangers or out of their boxes and laid them out on a piece of muslin on a large table. And then, for longer than I'd ever done with my own clothes, I studied them. I looked and looked: for tags and labels, any kind of brand or designer identification, fabric contents. I looked at their linings, scanned them inch by inch for tears, stains, and signs of wear—each a communication from its wearer in a previous life. I measured and photographed each piece from several angles, never very satisfied with my ability to recreate the life I saw and felt in the clothes. If librarians and archivists are eminently mockable for their obsession with the smell of books, I can profess that clothes are much more fragrant than paper. Traces of perfumes, soaps, mothballs, body odors. From the clothes I want to say I knew what Carson smelled like, but how could I ever describe it in words? I ran my gloved hands over the rich tweed skirt-suit in teal that looks like something she'd wear to meetings in New York with her publishers. Her long, pale lime-green wool A-line coat appears to be lined in emerald silk, but it is more likely polyester. She has several elaborately embroidered jackets and vests, things worn to theater and film premieres. Certainly Carson was never one for gowns. One item seems especially out of place, out of character: a gold lamé jacket with magenta lining that still has the Saks price tags on it, from all those years ago. It is the only item in the collection that looks unworn. Perhaps it was a gift.

The clothes in Carson's collection consist mostly of long coats, vests, and nightgowns, which, when I first encountered them, I didn't understand at all. Why would someone donate four cotton nightgowns to an archive? In a number of photographs, she wears the long red wool coat with embroidered gold trim, a garment with which I am deeply familiar. She called it her Russian coat, I think because it made her feel somehow "Russian," which could mean, knowing Carson's lifelong fascination with snowy climates, a person from a cold place. But it could just as easily suggest a person with a deep understanding of Anna Karenina. Carson refers frequently to Russian writers in her letters. I photographed the red coat from a ladder, I described it in metadata, I housed it in tissue and a box all its own. Like the clothes of our loved ones do, the coat began to resemble Carson, to signify a part of her. Years into this tunnel of research, I've solved the mystery of the collection of nightgowns and coats: she was a sick person. She wore, predominately, nightgowns, and often put a beautiful coat over them in photos. An interview with Rex Reed from 1967 describes how "she greets her guests in long white nightgowns and tennis shoes."

Carson revisits memories of her appearance, her elegance, in *Illumination*. Her friend in the last decade of her life, a

French woman named Marielle Bancou, whom Carson met on the bus from Nyack to New York, designed and made all of her "nightgowns and dressing robes," allowing her to be bedridden in style. If these were the nightgowns I catalogued, they are lightweight cotton in pale yellow, blue, and white, with simple lace collars, occasionally with ruffled sleeves. Some short sleeved, some long sleeved, one sleeveless. They have a childlike quality, something I may have worn to sleep in the summer when I was little. She writes about a gift she received from Dawn Langley Simmons, a close friend whom she met while visiting Edwin and John. Simmons gave Carson "one of her robes, a beautiful Japanese garment which I wear often. I love Japanese and Chinese robes and wear them on all state occasions. I have one, given to me by my cousin Jordan Massee, which is 2000 years old. It was worn in the old days on protocol visits to the dowager empress, and handed down from one generation to the next."

The age of this robe is the only lie I feel certain of in her autobiography. Having recently catalogued clothing only a few decades old, I'm highly skeptical that any fabric would remain intact that long unless elaborate preservation techniques were employed.

In Columbus, in the office of the Stark Avenue house, a silk kimono hung on a dressmaker's dummy under a sheet of plastic, and the director told me that this was the kimono she alleged to be 2000 years old. The first thing I did after

I was left alone in the house was remove this plastic. It is a dark, rosy pink, almost purple, embroidered all over with blue, pink, and green flowers and leaves. The wide beaded, embroidered lapel circles the collar, crosses, and closes at the side of the neck. I can see how wearing the garment on state occasions would make me feel distinguished, vaguely ancient. I had brought my sewing machine with me to Columbus, with coincidental plans to make a kimono, and this served as perfect inspiration. After uncovering the kimono, I opened the heavy, yellowing floral curtains, sat down at the massive desk, and looked across the room at the garment, at my own face in the mirror hanging beside it.

A year prior, surrounded, for the first time, by artists and writers at a residency in Vermont, I took to wearing a long black silk robe with magenta polka dots over my clothes every day. I had found it at a thrift store in Burlington. It was April 2015, and I'd driven from full Texas summer blue through midatlantic spring fog to a frozen, still snowing Vermont sky. The river outside my studio window slowly thawed over the course of the month, and by the end what had been solid ice was audibly rushing with snowmelt. In my first attempt to occupy the position of "writer" in public for any extended period of time, I felt the need to don what I deemed full writer drag: my robe, my knit hat, and my duck boots preceding any version of me, any writing at all, as I swept into and out of the dining room each day.

Toward the end of my stay in Vermont I sat in my robe at the desk in my studio surrounded by photos of McCullers's clothes that I had catalogued and all the photos of Annemarie I'd printed, a serial killer's lair. I pulled up the first draft of this book, which consisted of questions for the objects I'd catalogued, on my laptop so those who wanted to could read it on their tour around the writers' studios. I don't imagine anyone did. Writers' studios tend to be much less exciting than artists': no paint or clay, no half-assembled sculptures midroom, just a hard drive, maybe a notebook. A closed process. But this was my first studio, my first designated, if temporary, writing space, and I had papered the walls with lines I had written, one-sentence essays in india ink on paper.

I was sipping a plastic cup of red wine (having consumed half my bottle of bourbon the first night, at the bonfire, pouring it into a camping mug and continuing to drink because that's what I assumed a writer was supposed to do at a bonfire—What Would Carson Do?—and the next day, my first day to work, I was so ill I did nothing but sit in my studio's armchair in the fetal position, periodically spilling down the hall to throw up in the bathroom beside some poor poet's studio. I still don't know how those alcoholic writers do it). One of the older men in residence, a photographer with shoulder-length gray hair, came by my studio while I sat at my desk. He said he wanted to take my picture. He said it was for his wife, so she could see what I was wearing, I think to make it less weird that he was a man alone in a room with me taking my picture. I let him. It is one of those pictures of a writer at her desk, ones we see when Google Images searching for any writer, but I have never seen mine.

The desk in the Stark Avenue house's office was not Carson's, and in fact I find it odd that I have never seen mention of her desk. I think this one might have been Rita's at some point. Early on, Carson had several author photos taken sitting at—more often sitting on—a desk, usually out on the porch. Each piece of furniture that peoples the house in Columbus tells a story of its own: the white slip-covered couch where she wrote *Clock Without Hands*, her beloved blue armchair, the organ. When I picture Carson writing, I picture her reclined, looking out a window.

# Portals

The clothes are a kind of hinge or portal to the author's body, to her self and her self-representation. Even my item-level descriptions of the personal effects give away an investment that was perhaps too intimate for my role as intern.

"This straw hat has a black grosgrain ribbon band. The hat is misshapen, dirty, and worn, with tears on the side and top."

"This pair of socks is cable-knit with cream wool. Both socks show wear on the soles of the feet."

The other objects in the collection are a key to parts of her daily life, an inadvertently curated personal history I am left to decipher. What is the relationship between her bank books, her ink refills, and her mother's passport? Why this silver llama statue, why this handkerchief with a recipe for Irish coffee? As I worked, in my head I wrote questions for the objects I found, musings that kept nagging at me, unanswered.

# Item 8

Carson McCullers's mother's US passport was issued in 1951, when she was sixty-one. Carson embarked on a disastrous trip aboard the Queen Elizabeth in July, and the passport arrived from the State Department at Bebe's house in Nyack in October. The envelope and its contents found its way to the archive, which implies that Carson kept it with her own belongings. It reports that Marguerite Waters Smith was 5'8", with grey hair and brown eyes, born in Butler, Georgia. Her occupation is listed as "housewife." The passport bears a pink stamp indicating that it is not valid for travel to Japan, Okinawa, Bulgaria, or Czechoslovakia. This is irrelevant; the passport has no other stamps. Marguerite Waters Smith, were you planning a trip? Were you trying to go after Carson? Did you ever go anywhere? Her eyes look out from the black-and-white pasted-in photo, startled.

# Items 42–45

Oh Carson, darling, what were you thinking!? Always wearing your cotton nightgowns out on the porch. And imagine: being sick at a time when women didn't wear pants to bed.

# Items Unlocated

A handwritten note insists your eyeglasses went to Texas, along with the book you were reading and the ashtray at your bedside when you died. But Carson, I can't find them anywhere.

# Womanish

I spent hours looking at the photos of Carson in the Ransom Center, trying to understand something about her through her style. In some photos from her twenties, she wears a white dress, has long, waving hair past her breasts. In others, she wears a suit and a bob. *I want so badly to meet her!* I kept thinking, flipping through the folders. Clothes make visible what we feel or believe about ourselves, even if that identity is invisible to others. What we put on externalizes interior feeling, like a facial expression, but more intentional. This self-presentation takes as many forms as there are selves, and Carson's expression was by no means static.

Certain authors are known for their cultivated looks. Flannery O'Connor's cat-eye glasses, David Foster Wallace's damn bandanna, Gertrude Stein's extremely short bangs and long vests, Zadie Smith's head wraps. Carson had a look from the beginning. She often appears to have cut her own hair, possibly with pruning shears. Her bangs in early photos remind me of my own from childhood, when my mom used to cut them: short, crooked, and usually smushed down on part of my forehead from sleep. As Carson puts it,

> I wasn't downright homely, but I was no beauty no matter how [Mother] fussed over me. I would have to sit at the kitchen table and be primped. Since my hair was straight as a poker she tried to make little ringlets, and in so doing only mashed the hair of my head. Every morning before I went to school, she told me to say 'prunes or prisms,' because she said it made my mouth be set in a nice sweet way.

This scene from *Illumination* gives me flashbacks to picture days in grade school, when my mom would sit me in her bathroom and curl my stick-straight blonde hair under, even fashioning a sculptural half-moon with the bangs that protruded over my forehead. By the time I got to school, the curls would have fallen and the bangs would curve up and out, swooping salutes to impropriety. One year, second grade maybe, she got a comb stuck in my hair while curling. It was so stuck, my hair so fine and so acutely tangled, that it took her at least an hour—hours in my memory—to remove it, with so much pulling, so much passive aggression, that I threw up. I still can't untangle a necklace or anything small without feeling quickly nauseous. Carson's mom so badly didn't want her to wear glasses that she whispered the exam letters to her at the eye doctor.

Some of her baby photos show Carson dolled up as a little southern belle, a miniature princess swaddled in dresses and curls. There's one in particular where she wears a white dress, her hair very done, and sits in a wicker sleigh pulled by some poor dog. But when she escaped her mother's attempts to prettify her, Carson had her own style from very early on. I've mentioned the tie, the shorts. Eleanor Roosevelt writes, "attention and admiration were the things through all my childhood which I wanted, because I was made to feel so conscious of the fact that nothing about me would attract attention or would bring me admiration." I see in Carson's battles with her appearance the fact of growing up without the expected or desired traits of a woman, particularly a southern woman. The woman the world wanted her to be—with dainty features and demure affects—was deeply at odds with the woman she was.

I felt this when I was young, too, an unfittingness. Clothes have always been a defining part of my life, a mode of expression that helps mediate, or exacerbate, a sense of unbelonging. As a kid, from the time I was two or three, I had a penchant for changing my outfit several times a day. My parents called me a fashion statement. By the time I was in fourth grade, I brought a change of clothes with me to school in my backpack and changed in the bathroom before first period. I can only recall one of these outfits, a pair of leggings and a sweatshirt. I think, more than anything, I wanted to go out into the world without any comments or questions from my mom, or my brother, about what I had on. I wanted to determine my look. I still change clothes several times a day, altering parts of what I'm wearing to fit my activity or mood. For several years—third through seventh grade, maybe—I purposely mismatched my socks, coordinating them with my outfits. A bold, embarrassing choice, one that didn't win me new friends. But an expression, nonetheless. An assertion of difference. Of queerness, in retrospect. In the photos of Carson as a kid, in her shorts and knee-high argyle socks, I see a version of myself.

Biographers and critics have loved to describe Carson's wardrobe as "mannish," which I find kind of absurd. How many men wear lapels that large, cuffs that long? What about all the embroidery, the beading? Though now I am gender policing. Emily Hamer historicizes that "to be identifiable as a lesbian, as a woman who was not heterosexual, a woman had to distance herself from heterosexual femininity"—e.g., curls. "In a world of two genders," Hamer writes, "you can only distance yourself from conventional conceptions of femininity by gesturing towards masculinity." This analysis of historical lesbian dress makes sense, but I don't think it tells the whole story. I think lesbian style is much more nuanced than, "well, I'm not a traditional woman, so I'll put on this menswear!" The problem, as I see it, is how little common language we have to communicate androgyny, ambiguity. We rely on binary terms, masculine vs. feminine, to convey what is at heart both, or neither. I tend to think of Carson's look the way I think of Katharine Hepburn's, say, or Janelle Monáe's: not as that of a man but as that of a woman of a different order. Clothes offer a way to try on different identities, different manifestations of selfhood. They express more than gender, certainly more than binary gender, and more than sexuality, too. For Carson, they express her authorhood, her artist status, her illness, what made her feel most comfortable, what made her feel most dignified at even her least dignified moments.

In a photo taken in June 1958 by Richard Avedon, Carson wears her red Russian coat over a striped shirt. Her hair is a messy pixie, and her face is almost absent of expression, yet her eyes look deep into the camera. Avedon writes, "I remember her saying to me, 'I just want to look like Greta Garbo.'" When Carson was first coming into her own, it was a bold, scandalous choice for a woman to wear pants or shorts, one that Carson stuck to for most of her life. A headline from the 1930s reads "GARBO IN PANTS!" In *Harper's Bazaar* in 1948, a review of restaurants in Paris mentions that "Carson McCullers used to astound the Parisians by appearing for lunch in her blue jeans" at La Méditerranée, where Marlene Dietrich and Jean Gabin were "a daily twosome." I never know what to make of these coded but still quite obvious references to queer culture, to women toeing the line of femininity and straightness in public. Like when Carson and Tenn were featured on facing pages in a *Vogue* article called

"Incessant Prizewinners," Carson's Russian coat, her lapels and cufflinks, her cigarette, her gaze all a clear reflection of Tenn. Of the day Carson asked to look like Greta Garbo—whose name she pronounced "Greeta"—Avedon says, "Even though she was in pain, she couldn't have been giving more of herself. She had a complete understanding of the complexity and complicity between the sitter and the photographer and the fact that a portrait has nothing to do with the truth."

# On Exposure

All of these artifacts of Carson's life, fragmentary though they may be—her photos, her clothing, her paralyzed arm that she hid or did not hide, her will, her letters—can also be seen as a memoir. They offer ways of representing, exposing herself to the world. She writes to Mary in a letter after their second therapy session that she had worked all her life to expose or transmute the truth of her soul. Carson was not trying to hide her identity but to express it. She didn't write directly about herself, apart from what she wrote in her letters, and later, in *Illumination*, and I never came across a diary or mention of one. In her letters and in *Illumination*, her self-revelation, even her self-awareness on the page is incremental, sometimes painfully slow.

In April 1958, Carson said to Mary that she had bared her whole self to her, and that she had never shown so much of herself to anyone else, not Reeves, not Bebe, not Annemarie, not Oliver (Evans, who wrote an early analysis of her life and work), not Gypsy, or even Tenn. In her writing, as with her clothes, Carson attempted to make visible what she didn't have language to communicate.

Women writers and artists' negotiations with self-representation have at times become so fraught that they, like Italian novelist Elena Ferrante, choose to remove themselves completely from the public eye. Ferrante describes "the creative space that absence opened up for me. Once I knew that the completed book would make its way in the world without me, once I knew that nothing of the concrete, physical me would ever appear beside the volume . . . it made me see something new about writing. I felt as though I had released the words from myself." As in: the writing no longer had to do the work of creating a persona that corresponded with the author herself. This rejection of the expectation of authorial (self-) identification with her texts is already being challenged by those who would "out" Ferrante, tracking her identity through financial records. Like it or not, we leave traces of ourselves, our decisions, our interactions in the material world. And often we don't have control over them.

Ferrante, meanwhile, instead of an absence, has in recent years built a robust authorial presence, albeit a fictional one, through interviews, the publication of her editorial correspondence, and a weekly column. This fictional authorial persona is not so different from the authorial persona any writer contrives for herself. The "I" on the page is a construction, I am making her ("me") up and choosing which details, which aspects of her I reveal. And some of what comes across is beyond my choosing, gives me away when I'm not even aware of it. Ferrante has just fleshed out her character, her "I," given her room to speak and live and move in the world through correspondence written in her persona's voice.

She explains, "writing with the knowledge that I don't have to appear produces a space of absolute creative freedom. It's a corner of my own that I intend to defend, now that I've tried it. If I were deprived of it, I would feel abruptly impoverished." With the word "impoverished," Ferrante conjures an economy of freedom, of selflessness, of pub-liclessness. Of absence. Queer embodiment, like Carson's, like mine, requires a presence, a negotiation with public-ness. Invisible identities insist on being seen, or masked, or transformed, especially in the world of what Adrienne Rich called "compulsory heterosexuality." Women are straight unless they give themselves away. It is impossible to wrestle with/determine/express queer identity without some ne-gotiation with public scrutiny; presenting yourself to the world requires costumes and costume changes, which Car-son was well known for.

Writing, like clothing, can offer a way to express the unseen identities, longings, selves we carry—though this possibility is often taken as a certainty, used to suggest that writers leave absolutely everything of themselves on the page, their innermost experiences laid bare in prose. Marcel Proust claims, "that which enables us to see through the bodies of poets and lets us look into their souls is not their eyes, nor the events of their lives, but their books, precisely where their souls, with an instinctive desire, would like to be immortalized." As in: the work contains the person in some kind of entirety. But I have to question this presumed connection between the book and the unfettered soul. Carson's story of failed and unfinished attempts at her autobiography suggests that there are numerous obstacles between writing and self—soul—reification. It is impossible to reveal the full swath of the self on the page, in fiction or in memoir, just as it is impossible not to reveal parts of it.

And who is to say there is one soul, one story that ought to be immortalized? In practice, we are constantly revising the stories we tell about authors' lives and what they sought to communicate in their work. As readers we bring all of our own experiences and assumptions to bear on the author and what she writes. The author is immortalized, then, in a state of ongoing change, continuous retelling. And retelling inevitably brings to the surface some aspect of the teller and her motivations. Alive or dead, the author is a protean form, just as the self slips constantly beneath one's feet. Carson is changing as I write about her, and so am I.

# Conflation

Carson's face—jowly but expressive—reminds me of my own. I can't seem to help but find this overlap. It's happened since I was young: when I read something, or watch something, and identify with someone, I begin to imagine that I look like them. I feel their face moving in mine. When I was at the writing residency in Vermont and had access to a color printer, I printed a full-page photo of Annemarie, whom I was researching at the time—and then another, and another, because she is frankly stunning and so are the photos—and put them up on my wall. Something shifted, suddenly in my head I looked like her. I don't look like either of them, I'm sure. But I can feel my face changing as my allegiance shifts.

# The Hunt

In the fall of 2016, recently arrived in Santa Fe and grad-
ing hundreds of student papers each week for a terrible
online gig, I unexpectedly received an invitation off the
wait-list to work on my McCullers project for five weeks at
Yaddo. They wanted me to come the following week, and
they would pay for my plane ticket. I interpreted this as
a miracle. Yaddo was a dream of mine since I first started
writing, and a goal for inhabiting the places that were most
important to Carson. On my way to Vermont the previous
year I had gone out of my way to stop at Yaddo, driving
only as far as the sign that reads "Private area beyond here,"
whereupon I turned around, rebuffed. Yaddo is a posh
writers' and artists' colony in Saratoga Springs, New York,
about two hours from the city, that has welcomed novelists,
poets, composers, and visual artists since the 1920s. It was
a long trip to New York from my corner of the Southwest.
A dark train ride to Albuquerque for the red-eye to JFK,
and by the following morning I was falling in and out of
sleep on another train up the Hudson, leaves beginning to

change along its banks. As a taxi drove me for the second time in my life through Yaddo's gates, this time with permission to proceed past the two lakes and up the hill to the dark mansion, the driver, smirking in the rearview, wanted to know if they offered "turn-down service" for the artists. I told her I didn't think so, but I could see why she might.

My first night, late to dinner after falling asleep the second I arrived at my cabin, I took the empty seat beside a poet, a woman who kindly talked me through the procedures of a long and disorienting meal. She soon became one of my real friends. As is customary, a new arrival barely has a chance to eat dinner the first night: at the sight of an unfamiliar artist, the deeply isolated group of fifteen pounces and demands a detailed account of the stranger's life and work. Or at least this was the way of things during the late fall I spent in residence. I relayed the details of my project to the poet, keenly aware that every other person at the table was listening through their own conversations. I told her that I was writing about Carson McCullers and her relationships with women, and she said, "Oh, so she was a—?" And trailed off. A what? A lesbian? Was she?

After dinner, blissed out on roasted squash and bread pudding and homemade rum-raisin ice cream, I walked back to my cabin in the tall pines and paged through books on Yaddo and its history. I found myself scrutinizing the face of one woman in particular, Elizabeth Ames. Elizabeth was the director of Yaddo for nearly sixty years. Carson, age twenty-four, went to meet her after exchanging letters— Marjorie Peabody Waite, Elizabeth's sister, had set up the meeting after encountering Carson in Columbus. Waite immediately wrote to her sister, the sole force behind bringing artists and writers to Yaddo, asking her to "please meet this shy, sweet girl from Columbus who wants so badly to work at Yaddo, but who wouldn't dream of asking anyone to let her come." They were to meet in Elizabeth's hotel room. But when she arrived, Carson was so paralyzed with nerves that she had lost her voice and couldn't face her. She sat in the lobby, crying. Eventually, Elizabeth came down, scanned the lobby, and found Carson without ever having seen her before. She brought the unspeaking young woman up to her room and fed her tea, and eventually Carson came back to life. I imagine their first encounter like the department store scene in the movie *Carol*, where Carol holds all the cards and young Therese can barely talk.

Sitting up in my endless white bed, studying the books for photos of Elizabeth, I realized with a start that I was looking for clues. I was a sleuth. I was a huntress. I was hunting lesbians.

# Semantics

It has dawned on me, through researching how Carson lived in the '40s, '50s, and '60s, and through living as a lesbian every day, that each time a woman in the twentieth century is referred to by the epithets "widowed" or "unmarried," or when she is described as married but living away from her husband for a portion of the year—e.g., Georgia O'Keeffe— she is likely a lesbian to some degree or in some capacity.

Can it work this way, I wonder? Can a woman be part lesbian? So often the mainstream narrative gives us a straight woman who has the occasional wild affair or fling with a woman. Or one who went with women when she was young, in college perhaps. Or she has bisexual tendencies, say. "Ambivalences." Of Carson, they flag her "obsessive" crushes on various women and leave it at that. But I prefer the idea that we are all part lesbian, that we are lesbian to one degree or another. Is this semantics? To say that some part of every human being is a woman, and that part loves women, or has the capacity to do so. Jill Johnston: "All women are lesbians."

# Separate Bedrooms

It was at Yaddo, alone in her cottage, in November, 1942, that a telegram arrived informing Carson that Annemarie had died in Switzerland from brain injuries after a bicycle accident. She died, Carson tells Elizabeth in a letter, "with no one near." Carson was still writing *The Member of the Wedding* and finding it impossible to finish the book. She walked among Yaddo's enormous trees, grieving but also relieved. Carson decided to leave Yaddo and return to Columbus for the summer, to finish a new novel about a giantess and a hunchback, a mixed up hate-and-love affair between characters of indeterminate genders. From Columbus, Carson wrote to Elizabeth about how homesick she was for Yaddo, how stifling the summer months were in Georgia.

After their separation, and Annemarie's travels in Africa, Carson tells Elizabeth that her letters began to sound "certain and strong," and Carson could finally "think of her with peace."

Carson writes in *Illumination*, "I don't know of a friend whom I loved more, and was more grieved by her sudden death." In Columbus, "fall had finally come after the grueling heat, and I would walk to a hill near my house and pick up pecans and put them in my leather jacket."

With the other residents I took a tour of the Trask mansion, where writers are housed in the summers at Yaddo, which was closed in 2016 for renovations. The Trasks—Spencer, a banker, and Katrina (Kate), a poet and novelist—decided to make Yaddo a writers' and artists' colony after all four of their children died in different tragic circumstances (drowning, diphtheria). Spencer died in a train accident in 1909—while shaving on the train, the story goes—and Kate remarried a friend and her husband's, *ahem*, business partner, George Foster Peabody, just long enough to found Yaddo before she died. At the foot of the hill on which the mansion sits lies the rose garden Spencer had built for Kate, a maze of statues and mossy rocks.

The mansion, rebuilt once after a fire, is dark-gray stone and looks haunted and damp from the outside. The interior is not centrally heated, which made breakfasts in the dining room appropriately icy. On the mornings that I made it to breakfast before nine, when they stopped serving, I kept on my knit hat and huge red sweater and down vest, and sat at the designated quiet table, trying not to converse. I ate what amounted to three breakfasts: a bowl of oatmeal while

I waited for my poached egg and English muffin, plus a banana and yogurt to go. I savored every morsel.

In the rest of the house, closed off to us apart from this tour, all of the furniture and rugs were covered with white sheets. Ghosts, ghosts. Carson, I found out later, had to switch rooms when she was given the largest suite her second year at Yaddo. Kate Trask's room, painted pale pink and surrounded on three sides by windows with views of the mountains, gave her agoraphobia. Embarrassed, she swapped with her delighted neighbor without telling anyone. While I was there, residents staying in West House, where Kate and George lived together after Spencer's death, were thrilled to learn that their room had been formerly occupied by, say, Sylvia Plath or Langston Hughes. I myself was relieved to be housed in a brand-new cabin a bit away from the other buildings, the first resident to stay there. This took the pressure off, a pressure amplified by getting in off the wait-list and showing up after only a week to mentally prepare. It already felt like I had a lot to prove. The cabin didn't smell like anyone or anything except pine needles, which I kept finding in my bed each morning. I had room for all my thoughts, and none of the ghosts of anyone else's.

Life-size portraits of the four Trask children hang in the ballroom of the mansion. While everyone was studying the portraits, I noticed a large medallion on the wall that read "George Foster Peabody: Lover of Men." I learned on the tour that Kate and Spencer Trask kept separate bedrooms, Spencer's with its own entrance and staircase for his evening guests. Women? Men? Peabody? Or was Kate sleeping with Peabody while her husband was still alive? Were they all enmeshed? None of these questions were answered on the tour, though I asked. I also asked about Elizabeth, dying to know if she had some part in the romantic escapades of the Trask crew that the tour guide alluded to, but the guide affirmed my suspicions that Elizabeth is still an unknown quantity. She arrived at Yaddo after her sister Marjorie was adopted by Peabody. Marjorie was no child, but presumably Peabody's lover. Such adoptions were typical enough practice at the time. Beyond this, little is recorded about Elizabeth's personal life. But she was a force of knowledge and connection to artists and writers for much of the twentieth century.

Wandering the grounds one damp day, I found their circle of graves:

*George Foster Peabody, Ever Close Friend*
*Marjorie Peabody Waite*
*Allena Gilbert Pardee, Ever in the Circle*
*Elizabeth Ames*
*Spencer Trask, Guardian Spirit Ever Here*

And a tall memorial to Katrina Trask with candles on it, covered in leaves, at the center. They were a family of some kind.

# Androgyny

At Yaddo, Carson's gaggle widened when she found herself sitting at the queer table. The Table of the Sensitives ("dubbed by some presumably heterosexual wag," according to her friend Newton Arvin) introduced Carson to Lincoln Kirstein, a gay writer and ballet producer who knew one of her Brooklyn acquaintances, George Balanchine. Several biographers note that Carson sat at the queer table "unwittingly," but come on. Of *course* she found the queer table, whether or not she knew its designation outright. Imagining the scene brings to mind another moment in Lorde's *Zami*. Lorde, twenty years old, had recently arrived in Cuernavaca, Mexico, among a group of single and/or divorced women. "It never occurred to me that they were gay, or at least bisexual, themselves," Lorde writes. "I never suspected because a large part of their existence was devoted toward concealing that fact." Carson was in all likelihood more in-the-know about the sexual identities of the people she spent time with, but at first she may have instinctively gravitated there. Or, as a friend told me at a workshop once, "the queers always find each other, eventually."

Unlike life in Brooklyn, Yaddo had a strict privacy policy for its residents: no socializing, no visits with other guests until after four PM. Because meals are provided—breakfast and dinner in the mansion dining room, lunch picked up in a pail—Carson had no other obligations but to write and to attend dinner with the other guests. These rules, this schedule, applied to me during my stay. I am fairly certain they are still serving the same number of carrot sticks in each day's lunch pail that they've been serving since the 1920s. I wonder if Carson ate hers? Mine piled up in the mini fridge, and I left a few outside my front door for a downy mouse I saw huddled by the window out of the snow.

I found no queer table at Yaddo. We were a small enough group that we all ate together at one table most nights. However, I did find plenty of queers. On my first night, M, a gay painter from New York, walked his bike beside me as I headed back to the cabin. His new studio was even further out than the rest. In the dark, as we parted ways, he said that he had never imagined something he did would merit such bounty as this space. Neither had I.

Communities of artists are often queer, androgynous places. This is one reason I love them. In the few that I've participated in and, to an extent, in my current life in Santa Fe, I thrill at the comfort and ease of conversations centered around work and ideas. Hardly anyone is talking about their kids. I never feel the same pressure to explain what I do, or why I do it, nor do I have to explain who I am. Still, I flinched when M asked me my gender pronouns at dinner one night early on in my stay. He said it was because my Instagram profile read "a cat and his kitten," which referred to my cat, Elliott, and his kitten, Lou, but which he thought referred to me. I didn't take offense or interpret the question as a demand to account for myself. I already recognized M as kindred. I was just surprised, never having been asked before. When I got back from dinner, I stood in the bathroom and looked at myself in the mirror for a long time. I was smiling; I think I was kind of pleased. I remember it as a happy moment. New heights in androgyny achieved! But I also instinctively took it as a kind of flirtation. Surely he was hitting on me somehow. I realize later what a gendered response this is. I hadn't done a very good job so far at Yaddo with coming out to the other residents, telling them about Chelsea. I was more comfortable talking about Carson, so I kept coming out through my project. Despite the comforts of community, I felt isolated, unsure of my place in the group. It felt like all the other residents had helicoptered in directly from Skowhegan or MacDowell or some other swanky residency, not to mention they all had book deals and agents and galleries and MFAs and at least one had a Pulitzer Prize. They all seemed to know the same important people in New York, while I lived in Santa Fe in a loft with three cats and graded papers for a living. As usual, I felt like an outsider. I was craving affection and closeness, and for a moment I let myself think that maybe this painter was into me because he couldn't determine my gender without asking, though he was really being cautious, having just been at Skowhegan where he grew accustomed to asking for a person's pronouns. But the misperception made me see myself anew among strangers. I learned that I love that blur, the murk, the shift that androgyny in appearance allows, not as a means of escape from one label or another, but rather as a means of occupation. I occupy the category woman, and that category must expand to contain *me*. In all my outfits.

As a child, Carson changed her name from Lula to her middle name, Carson. Certainly her choice is the more androgynous name, one that is usually presumed to be masculine. "I'm writing a book about Carson McCullers," I say. "Oh, who's he?" most people reply. I wonder if that ambiguity was part of her choice, consciously or unconsciously, or if she just couldn't stand the name Lula. When I was in college, I started heading my papers with my first initial and last name, J. Shapland, an experiment with how my work might be treated when authored by a neutral— i.e., potentially masculine—name. I can't remember the outcome, only that I felt pleasantly not myself behind the initial at a time when I didn't know how to be myself.

As I flipped through her photos, I saw that Carson got more and more androgynous with age. Her hair only got shorter. She started out camping it up, in the costume of a grown man from the time she was a kid: she wore a huge tie and shorts and knee-socks and, in the photos, looks completely pleased with herself. Then came the lapels and cuffs, the pants, the look she's best known for. It's what she's wearing on her first book cover. The same look that got her in trouble with family friends when she came back to Columbus and dressing across gender lines wasn't funny or cute anymore, like it had been when she was a girl. People often mistook her for a man when they met her, even a boy. But as she got older, she leaned more toward silhouette-blurring, body- (and gender-) obscuring pieces, the pieces that introduced me to her when I catalogued them. Her woven vests, tunics, coats. And her nightgowns. The pieces she had made especially for her. I've started making my own clothes in the years since I began this project, frustrated that clothes in stores don't really look or fit or feel the way I want to look and feel. Which is: not masculine, not feminine, but a both that becomes other.

# They/Them

While at Yaddo I got an invitation from the Texas Book Festival to moderate a Q and A with Eileen Myles. I was several weeks in, and Yaddo was mist and trees and puddles and inch-thick layers of pine needles and leaves. Moss and ferns. Rain and rain. Lonely. I had just left Austin in June, in what felt like a frenzied rejection of the place and what it had come to represent to me: GOODBYE, Texas; goodbye, tech bros; goodbye academia and everything you stand for! But suddenly, from Saratoga Springs, Austin seemed very appealing, with its endless sunshine, tacos, good friends who'd known me longer than a week. Not to mention: Myles is my longtime hero. Each of their autobiographical novels—*Chelsea Girls, Cool for You, Inferno*—and their poems had gotten me through the past few years as I navigated my coming out, my decision to abandon an academic career, careerism in general. Eileen was and is a model for living on the outskirts of capitalism and convention. The last time Eileen was in Austin, I'd offered them a place to stay via Instagram. Though they didn't take me up on it, the inscription in my copy of

*Inferno* reads, "Thanks for the house." After about a minute of concern that the trip would take me out of my writing zone in residence, I said yes, absolutely. As usual, in the back of my mind I suspected I was getting unofficial access, that I was likely the last choice for this job. Who was I to interview an icon? And perhaps the underlying doubt, the one that made leaving the residency for a weekend so enticing: who am I to write about one?

A few days later, before I got in touch with Myles, I got an email from someone on the book-fest staff informing me that "Eileen goes by the pronoun 'they.'" This was news to me: the person who claimed to have run the first "openly female" campaign for president in 1992 was going by "they"? I even went so far as to let this bother me for a moment. My lesbian hero disidentifying from womanhood? How could I process this? But then the real concern blossomed: I had to be on stage with Myles in a few weeks and I could *not* fuck this up. On the phone with Chelsea and my friends, freaking out, we tried to practice using "they," but no one was successful every time. "She"s just slipped out.

In Austin, the night before Eileen's reading, I wrote out my introduction and questions: a script that would keep me sane and, I hoped, prevent any egregious pronoun errors. As Myles suggested I do in an email, I asked them what it means to be queer in being and in writing. I was too nervous to remember their exact words, but Myles answered

something along the lines of *constant shifting, the ever new.*
This part I do remember. Eileen: "I've earned better words
than 'Miss.'"

# Confidantes

Back in my cabin, I needed to know more about Elizabeth Ames, but Yaddo's archives had recently been moved off the grounds to the New York Public Library. Pat, one of the two residents in her seventies, was driving to the city the following week and offered me a ride. Again I left my comfortable cottage and my free meals, my daily poached eggs to order—my dad told me on the phone it sounded like I was in assisted living—on a lead to find yet another lesbian, or someone I presumed to be one.

I had never been to the New York Public Library, any branch, even during my lonesome, clove-cigarette fueled stint on Water Street. Pat dropped me as close as she could get to the main library without getting trapped by traffic, despite my offer at each block to jump out. She was one of my residency mothers. After signing up for my third new library membership that month, I spent several hours rifling through Ames's papers in the manuscript room: her notebooks, her letters, Yaddo records. She had an entire notebook devoted to pasted-in poems that she had cut from the newspaper or retyped, a catalog of lost and semi-lost women writers. Ann Rutledge, Edna St. Vincent Millay, Margaret Widdemer, Jessie Rittenhouse, Katherine Mansfield, Elinor Wylie, Ruth Fitch Bartlett, Lizette Woodworth Reese, Gwendolyn Haste. How many of these do you recognize? (My friend Laura, a queer scholar, in response to this list of names: "Definitely a lesbian.") Ames detailed her studies of Chinese philosophy, world religions, architecture, all in pencil. Nothing emerged about Ames herself or her personal life, though I did come across her lists of the writers she had invited into residence and where they were housed at Yaddo. And several menus, lists of recipes. The food at Yaddo has a long history. Each night at dinner, they serve fresh bread with butter balls, made by the kitchen staff using wooden paddles. I still don't really know why. Tradition, like the carrot sticks. Nourishment. In Ames's notes, I read *Whipped cream, stiff.*

I requested a reel of microfilm that the records indicated contained some correspondence between Ames and McCullers. Vaguely disappointed with what I'd found so far—a few brief logistical exchanges with writers, a $10 phone bill to James Baldwin—I made the trip out of the manuscript room and down six flights of marble stairs to the frigid microfilm bunker. I felt odd carrying the reel such a long way in my hand. What if I dropped it? Or just walked out of the building? I considered putting it in my pocket for safety, but didn't want it to look like I was stealing. Archives always conjure this mix of overwhelming constraint and bewildering freedom for me. The environment is at once completely controlled, down to what kind of paper and pencil you can use, and totally unrestricted: your hands turning the pages of someone's letters and notebooks, your mind and heart reading them.

Positioned in front of a viewing machine the size of my body, I began to scroll through the letters, past some correspondence between Elizabeth and other writers. Then I got to Carson. To get a sense of the scope, how many letters I would need to scan, I tried to scroll to the end. I scrolled for hours that afternoon, and gathered and saved nearly two hundred pages of letters, clippings, and manuscript drafts from Carson to Elizabeth. After their initial meeting in the hotel lobby, they had become close friends. In the letters, Carson is frank and open with Elizabeth about her love and affection for her, as well as her periodic romances with other women in New York, none of which appear in the biographies or anywhere else in Carson's writing. With Ames, she felt she could be honest about who she was—or at least whom she loved—to an accepting, understanding confidante.

In an undated letter she writes that she has "met someone," and that their friendship "has about it an emotional quality that has disturbed me." She goes on to describe a woman she met in New York, explaining that their relationship has "a tension" to it that is unlike her other friendships. While she mentions that the relationship is not necessarily "a sexual one," she also says that her feelings for her close friends are her most significant "emotional experience[s]."

She follows this vulnerable revelation to Elizabeth with a request to come back to Yaddo for the winter, and closes by telling her, "Today I gave in to our common vice. I ate about half a pound of chocolate, then gobbled up a box of nasty little cookies." Carson wrote to Elizabeth when she was down and confused, scarfing down chocolate and in love with a lady director.

As she moved back and forth between New York, Yaddo, and Columbus throughout the 1940s, Carson continued to write to Elizabeth, detailing her struggle to finish *Wedding* after Annemarie's death and amid ongoing drama with Reeves.

Carson tells Elizabeth that at Yaddo and in Columbus, she can feel things "deeply" without being "tormented" as she is in the city. She feels "at peace," she says, and "happy in my room alone, shut in with my wedding."

It's a wedding that Frankie longs to join in the novel: not a person or a relationship, but the public, sanctioned manifestation of love as she understands it. None of Carson's books portray out lesbians, but *Wedding* certainly comes closest. In *Illumination,* Carson recalls the moment she finally understood what *Wedding* was really about. Running down the street in the midst of a house fire, Carson told Gypsy, "'Frankie is in love with the bride of her brother and wants to join the wedding.'" This straightforward statement of Frankie's love for another woman will be transfigured in the book into a feeling that she can neither comprehend nor express, and will manifest not as love for the bride but as a desire to join the wedding. Each of her ideas for the book suggest a girl's desire and love for a woman as *Wedding*'s overt subject. Prior to her house fire realization, Carson writes that "Frankie was just a girl in love with her music teacher, a most banal theme." I wonder if she really felt the subject "banal," or if she didn't feel like she could write directly about a woman's love for another woman. Either way, Frankie's longing grows out of Carson's attempt to address unspoken lesbian desire.

To Elizabeth, she writes, "I suppose this book is my autobiography."

# The High Line

I walked to Pat's apartment along the High Line to catch a ride back to Saratoga Springs, back to the place where I felt I could feel deeply, without disruption. A billboard-sized copy of Zoe Leonard's poem "I Want a President" was pasted up on the wall, in front of which an older couple was taking their photo. The first line reads "I want a dyke for president," followed by "I want a person with aids for president and I want a fag for president and I want someone with no health insurance . . ." The 2016 election was a few days away. I was walking along thinking about our first woman in office, how ready I felt for that, though the campaign had been a nightmare. Carson would have been furious at the rampant racism, unable to stand the misogyny directed at Hillary Clinton, or so, deep inside my version of her mind, I imagined. It was hard to believe it was really happening, but I felt somehow entitled to a woman president. Now, years into Trump's presidency, I am learning, yet again, that history does not progress, does not move forward, cannot be understood as some sort of

142

trajectory we can draw between past and future that goes through the present.

Like when I look at the history that surrounded Carson, all I can see in our present moment is a scatterplot of points and a best-fit line that never quite catches any of them. A lot of people talk about Carson McCullers as "ahead of her time," given, I presume, her empathetic writing about gay men, interracial love, racism, and disability in the 1940s and '50s. But perhaps, in light of a recent election and its aftermath that signal the ongoingness of racist and homophobic and misogynistic and ableist bigotry even during political moments that seem progressive, it feels more accurate to say that she was just plain empathetic to human differences. That it has nothing to do with history, with "the times," with generation. When I read Carson's fiction, it is clear that empathy is a choice a person makes, moment to moment, in how they approach other people. On the page and off.

In the election's wake, back at Yaddo, I stayed in bed and barely ate anything, falling asleep for three hours in the middle of the day for no reason but grief. I'd been dipping into a volume called *The Years and Hours of Emily Dickinson*, which uses her letters, diary entries, and newspapers to map her day-to-day life, an attempt to include every single event that has been recorded. A tick-tock. I guess that's one way to write a biography: no writing at all, just transcription of events in strict chronological order without comment or explanation. Perhaps that is the ideal biography. I've been thinking historically about being a woman artist or a lesbian at a time in the past when people openly hated or denied or refused to take women seriously, when people didn't really even believe women artists or lesbians were real, or that they mattered. As my friend, lesbian artist Harmony Hammond, writes of coming up in the 1960s and '70s, "to be both a woman and an artist was considered a contradiction of identities." And now suddenly I have no choice but to face the possibility that this moment is no different from Carson's 1950s or Emily's 1860s or Harmony's 1970s, that history recurs or continues to be the same conversation, the same story, with the same limits, revised according to one's political views.

It makes me think that there will never be a time when women or lesbians are real—when we call them by name, use the right words to recognize them/ourselves. It's analogous to the concept of coming out, for the oft-cited reason that you never *stop* coming out as a queer person; every time you meet someone new you must find a way to broach the topic or risk closeting yourself. But also because I don't feel like I was ever actually *in*. I feel more like, growing up in a conservative, reticent community, I just didn't know—for lack of example and lack of vocabulary—what I was, what I could be, that I could love women and still be myself. All I had was Zelda Fitzgerald. I'm drawn to Carson's story and to her fictions of growing up in places that feel cut off, isolated, conservative compared to some other world out there that one can't quite access. Like when she asked Reeves what lesbians were, how they acted. It makes sense that February House and Yaddo meant so much to Carson, and came up so frequently in her therapy sessions with Mary even decades later. Communities of queers, of artists, can be tiny but mighty worlds in which to form a self.

Giddily picking out places we might live when we escaped Texas, Chelsea's hometown, Birmingham, made the short list. But when we visited, I noticed that everywhere we went—every restaurant, store, bar—we were the only couple that wasn't visibly straight. We couldn't see a community where we'd belong, and the idea of starting our own seemed too daunting. Not so in Santa Fe. As we house hunted at a distance, just about every Craigslist ad for a rental came with a woman landlord: metalsmiths, weavers. We moved to Santa Fe in part because of the stereotype of women living on their own in New Mexico, which reflects a long history of lesbian artists and writers. Our current landlord, Jan, wove tapestries for Judy Chicago's *Dinner Party*. She calls herself an Amazon warrior.

And the significance does not escape me that, as I write this, I am living—housesitting—at Harmony's, occupying the home of one of the greatest lesbian artists of our time, surrounded by books and paintings and postcards and photos that all confirm her love for women. The objects make it real.

# Threesomes

Carson struggled with *Wedding* throughout the early and mid 1940s, but in the meantime, moving between Columbus and Yaddo, she quickly began and finished a new manuscript. The idea for *The Ballad of the Sad Café* came during one of her outings in Brooklyn and took shape in the following months.

She recalls the time she spent on Sands Street, cavorting with the memories of Walt Whitman and Hart Crane, and the night she saw "a remarkable couple" who would serve as the "illumination" for her next book.

The main character in *Ballad*, the formidable Amelia, who runs the local café, presents as a full-grown dyke. Separated from her husband, to whom she was married for ten days before she rejected him (whereupon he beat her, went on a crime spree, and wound up in the state pen), she falls in some kind of love with a gentle little man who comes to town claiming to be her cousin Lymon. Her ex-husband returns and the two men gang up on Amelia, ransacking her store and leaving her, again, alone. Some have suggested that Cousin Lymon might be a rendering of Truman Capote, whom Carson helped introduce to the New York publishing world. She convinced her editor for *Ballad* at *Harper's Bazaar*, Mary Lou Aswell, the longtime partner of the artist Agnes Sims, to publish Capote's early work. Later on, Carson grew to resent Capote for imitating her work, and the two refused to share the same air.

At the time of *Ballad*'s writing, after she had divorced Reeves, Carson received an unusual marriage proposal, by letter, from their mutual friend David Diamond. Carson, who had just finished reading sexologist Havelock Ellis's autobiography *My Life*, imagined he proposed a marriage of convenience, like Ellis's with his wife, Edith. Edith Lees was a lesbian, or what Ellis referred to as an "invert," and she had relationships with women throughout their marriage, with her husband's knowledge. David had something more intimate in mind in marrying Carson, and Carson flat-out refused him. Carson told David that she wished Reeves could have understood her as Havelock understood Edith. She seems not to have had the book's tragic ending—Edith winds up (like Zelda, like Annemarie, like so so many women) in an asylum—in mind when she said this. Reeves had also read Ellis many years earlier, hidden in the back room of a Georgia library. Havelock and Edith's lavender marriage, which served to conceal one or both partners' queer sexual and romantic practices, may have been the marriage Carson longed for with Reeves, for whom, she told David, she had no remaining physical attraction.

At a time when sexuality was not well understood, Ellis's autobiography of unconventional marriage was a vital source of definition for both Reeves and Carson. Ellis wrote a foreword to Radclyffe Hall's novel *The Well of Loneliness* for its 1928 publication, a novel in which the protagonist refers to herself as an invert. Carson calls herself an invert in her response to Diamond's letter, drawing the term either directly from Ellis or from Hall's novel. Diamond's proposal came in 1941, and the Kinsey reports, which first suggested sexuality and gender as changing and continuous spectrums rather than fixed designations, would not be published until 1948.

Inversion theory understood gender as a strict binary, in which homosexuality could only be interpreted as a reversal of anatomical gender traits. Many people in the early twentieth century were reading Freud and Ellis and taking their emphases on binaries and opposites in gender and sexuality as gospel. Homosexuality was just beginning to formulate as an identity in opposition to heterosexuality, which itself only became a concept during this time period. While it was okay in some circles to experiment with non-heteronormative sexual relationships, Freud and others made it clear that long-term homosexual behavior, especially at the exclusion of heterosexual partnership, was a kind of pathology or reversal of "normal" gender and sexual expression, a disease that had to be eradicated. At the time, perhaps these ideas had more purchase: feminism had not yet exposed Freud as a raving misogynist, nor had the implications of Ellis's horrifying affinity for eugenics fully revealed themselves.

While Carson was away from New York, Reeves moved into David's apartment in Rochester. All evidence suggests that theirs was a romantic and physical relationship. Carson stopped communicating with David altogether, fearing interaction with him might bring Reeves back into her life. When *Ballad* was published, she told David, "Darling, *The Ballad of the Sad Café* is for you."

# Recliner

I caught a glimpse of myself framed in the floor-to-ceiling window of my studio at Yaddo: pajama clad, cross-legged in the leather recliner with a cup of coffee beside me. I spent nearly the entire five weeks in this chair, with a stack of books beside me and on my lap, my notebook nearby, and I slept and awoke, and I felt frailer than usual. One day I brought the white quilt from my bed and draped it over me, and that became the new routine. I watched through the window, down toward the lake below, one of the four lakes named for each of the four Trask children. Soon it was full of leaves and it was hard to tell where the water began. The trees were so tall that I had plenty of time to watch each leaf fall, fall, fall all the way down, and one day when I looked out the leaves had turned to snow.

When Carson was away from Yaddo, she wrote to Elizabeth about how badly she missed the "certain serenity and discipline" she found there. "All during this year," she wrote in an undated letter from Columbus, "I shall imagine what you all are doing, and think about snow, and the green lakes frozen. It will be as though part of myself is there."

Writer Helen Vendler says that, during her time at Yaddo, thought became a place to dwell, rather than a linear process. This room made of thought brought her back to being fifteen, when she first began writing what she thought of at the time as "real" poems. I can relate: I felt most in residence with my own thoughts when I was an adolescent. And I think I'm always trying to get back to this space, this intensity and the freedom to explore it, that Carson writes about in *Wedding*. This space is writing, it is a room, it is an armchair, a tree house, it is the nourishment I found in mugs of hot cocoa I made in my cabin, with scoops of healing pink Himalayan salt that Pat brought me from her apartment.

Patricia Highsmith, lesbian novelist, called her two months at Yaddo her "summer of peace." She was only in residence once, in 1948, and no written record of her stay remains in the Yaddo archives. Nowhere in Elizabeth's notes does she appear. At Yaddo, she wrote the bulk of *Strangers on a Train* and spent plenty of time drinking in Saratoga Springs after working hours. She found a queer community of her own while in residency, befriending the gay novelist Marc Brandel and talking to him at length about sexuality as they walked the grounds. (He soon proposed, four different times, hoping to establish a marriage of convenience.) When Highsmith died, unbeknownst to anyone at Yaddo,

it was revealed that she had named Yaddo the sole ben-
eficiary of her estate: $3 million at the time, plus any fu-
ture royalties, including proceeds from films made from
her books, like *The Talented Mr. Ripley* and *Strangers on a
Train* and, recently, *Carol*. Nestled in my brand-new cabin,
I liked to imagine that the heated floors and walls of windows were derived directly from *Carol*'s box office success.
Chelsea and I listened to the audiobooks of *Strangers on
a Train* and *The Price of Salt* on road trips when we were
first in New Mexico, enthralled by Highsmith's ability in
both books to render creepy queer romance as transcon-
tinental crime drama. She published *The Price of Salt*, on
which *Carol* is based, in 1952 under the pseudonym Claire
Morgan, concerned, she wrote in 1990, that she might be
labeled a "lesbian book writer" if she used her real name.
She was also trying to protect the people on whom she
based her characters. It's her only novel that charts a lesbian
romance, and it's still credited as one of the first lesbian
novels of the era to end happily—rather than with the typical death or straight marriage. I wonder if Carson read it.

Carson and Highsmith knew each other, though they
weren't close. Highsmith went to visit Carson in Nyack in
1949, toting along two of the women she was currently
sleeping with, and they spent the afternoon with Carson,
Bebe, Rita, and Reeves. While staying at Rosalind Con-
stable's house on Fire Island in 1950, Highsmith met up
for drinks at Duffy's Hotel with her current lover Anne,

February House-mate Jane Bowles, "her agent Margo's girlfriend," gay composer Marc Blitztein, and Carson. In 1953, Highsmith learned from lesbian art gallerist Betty Parsons that Carson had "fallen madly" in love with one of Highsmith's ex-lovers, the London psychoanalyst Kathryn Hamill Cohen, and had been waiting around London for three months hoping Kathryn might live with her. Like so many lesbians, then and now, Carson and Highsmith's paths and love interests intersected repeatedly. Each of the women mentioned in this paragraph could easily have a book written about her just like this one.

Carson was in residence at Yaddo six times throughout the 1940s and one last time in 1954. Once, when she fell ill at Yaddo and went home to Columbus, she left behind all her summer clothes, "(my overalls and shorts etc)." She also left behind a book checked out from the Lucy Scribner Library at Skidmore college up the hill, where I spent many of my afternoons picking out stacks of books about Carson and Highsmith and the 1940s that I would cram into my backpack and tote back down the hill on one of Yaddo's blue bikes, through piles of orange leaves.

Everyone's favorite Yaddo anecdote, as I learned from talking to other residents, each of whom came to Saratoga Springs with their own mythology about Yaddo and its history, is (apart from John Cheever's continual nudity and exposures to unsuspecting guests) the story about Carson

McCullers chasing after Katherine Anne Porter. It's a good one. As the legend goes, young, desperate Carson became obsessed with the elegant, older southern writer and tried again and again to approach her. Repeatedly rebuffed, Carson came to Katherine's cabin and laid herself down in the entry way, where she waited for her to emerge for dinner. When Katherine finally came out, she stepped over Carson's prone, pathetic body and the two never spoke again.

Katherine Anne Porter was avowedly repulsed by "Lesbians." When she refers to them in writing she capitalizes the "L" as though referring to some kind of mythological monstresses. It wasn't uncommon to think of lesbians as monsters or "sickos" in the post WWII years; so many of the images of lesbians that circulated in pulp novels codedly, intentionally made them out to be gorgons, diseased, hardly human. I naturally presume Katherine was repulsed by her own fear, by her own self. Thou doth protest too much, Kate. While all the versions of this story I've read make Carson out to be obsessed with Katherine, what if all she really wanted was a mentor? A friend?

# Ontological Destabilization

After the election, my loneliness magnified. I had been surrounded by Trump lawn signs in Carson's neighborhood in Columbus during the primary the previous spring, but I never saw them as anything but a desperate clinging to conservative worldviews that were clearly dying out. The lawn signs were delusional. At Yaddo in October, we read aloud, over breakfast, from the *New York Times*, a paper I slowly began to resent balking at the continuing stupidity of the campaign to elect a reality TV star to the highest public office. Jenny, my other residency mother, read us the groping stories, appalled. One day a Trump sign appeared at the entrance to Yaddo, right outside, and after dinner we marched as a group to rescue our creative haven from such an insult. We were too absorbed in our work, in our collective solitude, to recognize the bubble for what it was.

When it burst, I didn't just lose Yaddo but the legible boundaries of my self. The world outside my cottage, my woods—the world I ingested primarily through the internet—was suddenly unrecognizable as a place where I could belong, not because it had changed, but because I was now required to see it for what it was. The night I watched the results come in at the home of Yaddo's director, who handed out her daughter's stuffed animals for us to hug as the dread wore on, Chelsea texted, "What's going to happen to us?"

I processed my feelings alone, in bed, eating peanut butter cups, and on the phone with friends around the country as I walked the woods, shocked that the trees were still there. I took out my fear and confusion on the other residents at dinner, insisting at every turn, "Actually, it's even worse than that," and then explaining how it was worse, my ruminations on the stream of news I scrolled through with one eye open transformed into the hard truth it was my duty to expose. I felt cut open and kept recalling a passage from *Member of the Wedding* when the news of the war and the world's instability hits Frankie for the first time.

> Frankie stood looking up and down at the four walls of the room. She thought of the world, and it was fast and loose and turning, faster and looser and bigger than it had been before. . . . Finally she stopped looking around the four kitchen walls and said to Berenice: 'I feel just exactly like somebody has peeled all the skin off me.'

One's self and one's world constantly shift and alter, and all we know for sure about either is that they are never the same, but this doesn't stop us from acting as if they are continuous, stable. As if the future will follow logically from the present, as if the present is something we are really able to know. In an essay published after the election, Bosnian American novelist Aleksandar Hemon writes, "if the world and life are one, if I am my world, as Wittgenstein suggested, then the rupture in the solidity of that world transforms who I am, regardless of my will and intention." When the older artists and writers around me at Yaddo saw my panic as I felt the world remade, they tried to reassure me: he won't follow through on his campaign promises, he'll be impeached, you'll see. I refused their stabilizations. "If he's impeached," I snarled, "then we get a president who believes I should go through conversion therapy, who believes I might need electroshock."

When I finally came out—eight years after the walk in the botanic gardens, two years after my narrative breakdown— it felt like an embrace of this kind of rupture. To open my self, my life to queerness was to eradicate the carefully hewn path that had lain before me since I knew anything: that I would marry some man, have kids, a house, a legible future. Queerness required me to throw legible futures out the window. It took me some time before I was able to do this. When I finally did, I marked the occasion with a tattoo. I didn't even fully know it was queerness that I was embracing at the time, but when I went with my friend Jordan to Atomic Tattoo around the corner from the Ransom Center, I knew that a tattoo would distinguish the person I used to be or thought I was from the person I was becoming. It would be a marker. I got a line tattooed around my left bicep, its two ends sliding past each other without meeting.

Carson wrote much of *Wedding* in the summer of 1943 at Yaddo after Annemarie's death, after Carson's own world and self had split open. In therapy, after Carson finally tells her Annemarie story all the way to the end, Mary says to her, "You stand at the threshold of really coming into your own, and I would say it's about time."

# Googling

Struggling to make headway on the project while feeling myself invalidated, I devoured book after book from Yaddo's library of titles authored by former writers-in-residence. I spent hours in this room reading and learning who all had visited and what they had written here. No one else ever came in, so I was free to read and sit out of the rain and cry at my leisure. I devoured Natalie Goldberg's *Writing Down the Bones* in one sitting. Goldberg's book struck a chord in me. Writing is a physical act, she insists, a movement of the body. I finished the book and reread the author's bio on the back cover, then began to Google. Within a minute I was typing "Natalie Goldberg lesbian" into the search bar. I cannot tell you the number of times I have typed this search with different women's names. I learned that yes, indeed, Goldberg has had a woman partner. But as far as this simple search told me, Goldberg does not identify publicly as a lesbian or bisexual or talk about her partner anywhere besides the one interview where she mentions her. I called Chelsea and before I knew it I was railing about how can even *Natalie Goldberg*—who lives, I might add, in our queer little Santa Fe—be closeted?

I've since read her other books, and she does write about her women partners quite openly. I also met Natalie— Nat—and learned that reading *The Ballad of the Sad Café* in ninth grade changed her life. She always thought it was because Amelia was such a strong woman character, but when she found out Carson was queer, she realized it went much deeper than that.

# Preaching

So it isn't about "Is Carson a lesbian?" or "Carson is a lesbian" or "What *is* a lesbian?" What I want to know is, how have lesbians gotten by and had relationships and found love and community? What does that look like? One answer: we don't really know. If we—writers, historians, biographers—can just start acknowledging the lesbian parts of ourselves and others, maybe we can start to know what it is. What it is to love women. But please, no more demands for certain kinds of proof, no more "doesn't count unless—" bullshit. Don't tell me there's just not enough evidence. Let's call a lesbian a lesbian. Call yourself a lesbian if you've ever loved women. Loved another woman. Period. You loved your mother? Lesbian.

It's all well and good for me to say this now, but what have I been doing all along if not looking for proof? When I found what I was looking for, I had no clue what to do with it, what it meant. Queer histories often take the form of lists, of calling out and naming kindred spirits. This practice has largely gone out of vogue, as labeling a person's gender or sexual identity, past or present, is fraught with complexities—what did that person call themself and what did it mean at the time? Is it best to call a person queer, or to specify? Is labeling always an essentializing force? As Maggie Nelson insists, "the best way to find out how people feel about their gender or their sexuality—or anything else, really—is to listen to what they tell you, and try to treat them accordingly, without shellacking over their version of reality with yours." Perhaps in calling Carson queer, calling her a lesbian, I am shellacking, setting her on my terms despite my desire to give her space in her own words. By including her words, I make them my own.

But there's a part of me, a defiant and somewhat juvenile part, that still wants the list. It's not all that important to me to define what it is to be a lesbian—*constant shifting, the ever-new*—but I can't help but want to know who else is at the table with me, who I can call kin.

# List of Carson's
# Possible Girlfriends

Joy Fleming

Helen (childhood friend)

Louise Dahl-Wolfe (photographer, took Carson's author photos in 1941 and in 1961)

Unidentified woman "obviously a friend of Carson's in France"

Hilda Marks

Miss Minnie (Jack Dobin's mother)

Ida Reeder (Carson's last nurse)

Marielle Bancou

Helen Johnson Visone (possibly "Helen from childhood")

Kay Boyle (named her daughter Faith Carson)

Annemarie Clarac-Schwarzenbach

Edith Begner

Miss Kathleen McCoy, 248 So Pryor Street, Atlanta, Georgia (postcard addressed, never sent)

Jane Bowles

Gypsy Rose Lee

Elizabeth Bowen

Katherine Anne Porter

Dr. Mary Mercer

Mary Tucker

Vera

Elizabeth Ames

Kathryn Hamill Cohen

# Other Likely Lesbians

Rita

Jane Warwick, to whom Rita left one-third of her estate

Rita's "friend-roommate" Merle Berlant

Carson's Aunt Isabel, the nun

Cheryl Crawford and Ruth Norman

Carson's Aunt Tieh

Virginia Spencer Carr

Karen Blixen (aka Isak Dinesen) and "her dear friend and secretary, Clara Svendsen"

Edith Sitwell

Ethel Waters

# Second Marriages

Reeves went to war in November 1943 and was wounded at Normandy the following year, while Carson was at Yaddo. That same summer, she received news that her father had died. She returned to Columbus for the funeral in August. Her mother refused to go inside the house on Stark Avenue after he died. Carson, Bebe, and Rita all moved together to an apartment in Nyack, New York, a town on the Hudson River where Carson would spend most of her remaining years.

Bebe's unwillingness to return to their Georgia home makes more sense in light of a 2003 revelation in Virginia Carr's introduction to the reissue of her 1975 biography. In *Illumination*, Carson had written, "in the middle of these years of fury and disaster my father suddenly died of a Coronary Thrombosis. He died in 1944 at his jewelry store." According to Carr, this is not at all the truth. She writes, "both the coroner and the obituary in the local newspaper reported that Mr. Smith had died in his jewelry shop of a heart attack. But I learned later that he had died from a self-inflicted gunshot wound to the head—Bebe, his wife, 'insisted that we tell no one.'" It is another rewrite, one that makes it into Carson's own retelling of her life. She does not speak of her father's death to Mary in the therapy transcripts.

Reeves started sending Carson letters while he was abroad, and though their exchanges don't follow reciprocally—each would often receive a batch of letters from the other written over several months—together they wrote sixty letters in total between 1943 and 1945. I chafe at the possessiveness that creeps into each of Reeves's passes at affection. "You are my own Precious Carson and I don't believe any one has ever been loved as much as I love you." He insists that they "just need to live together for about five years straight without interruption," and spends at least a paragraph of each letter contemplating where they might live after the war. It seems to be his way of coping with the fear that he might not come home. As the letters continue, he sounds desperate, cloying. "Nothing I do or feel is good unless I can share it with you." He writes of and underlines his "great fear . . . that the imaginary friend would come between us to the extent that I would be destroyed." More than love and affection, and certainly more than their future relationship, Carson's letters to Reeves are frantic with worry over his immediate well-being and his safe return. Often she writes in impatience at not having had word from him recently, not knowing whether he is alive, and begs him to write immediately. The war and the threat of losing Reeves seem to provoke enormous anxiety in Carson, and she expresses it by wondering what he is doing and telling him her thoughts on what she's been reading—Henry James, William Faulkner.

Reeves came back from the war, wounded and decorated, in February 1945, and Carson recalls in *Illumination*, "as soon as he returned to Nyack, he immediately started a barrage to make me marry him again. I said, '[Second] marriages are so vulgar . . . We're much better as friends, without marriage.' Marriage, however, was his motive." Elizabeth tried to warn Carson off, seeing the "great danger in a remarriage." Carson recalls that Reeves's letters throughout the War returned repeatedly to the subject of marriage, though she felt unenthusiastic about the idea. She tells Mary that if she and Reeves had been able to be friends, without possessiveness or dependency, his life might not have ended so tragically. But Reeves would not take friendship for an answer. In March, unconscionably, they remarried in a civil ceremony in New York. This second marriage seems to be the basis for biographers of Carson to presume that theirs was a great love, a lifelong relationship that was constitutive of both their identities.

Why Reeves? Why a second time? Their first marriage showed that Carson wasn't satisfied with being a wife for very long. I wonder if, after losing Annemarie, and then her father, in the shadow of war, it was a way of trying to hold onto some kind of legible identity. I come back to her protracted becoming: if she was still trying to figure out who she was, what she wanted, it isn't so hard to be talked into a life, a self, an identity. It can seem easier to stop asking "who am I?" altogether. I find myself questioning, too, the line here between manipulation and consent. How much of Carson and Reeves was really love? Can love and manipulation co-exist? Manipulation and consent? He was violent—emotionally and psychologically abusive. What once seemed like passion morphed into rage, resentment, brutality. No love exists in a vacuum, no matter how much it feels like it does. It is filtered by all the loves we've ever read about, witnessed, watched, lived. Its definition is given by use (to nod at Wittgenstein). Love changes in each phase of a relationship, each day, even. As we, too, change constantly. Nor can love be proven. It's more complicated, harder to see than a ring, a marriage license, a description of any physical encounter.

Reeves's determination seems to be the primary force behind Carson's decision. Elizabeth told her that in the aftermath of the war "girls everywhere are marrying and remarrying men they would not have married otherwise." In fact, more marriages occurred during these years than in any other period of US history, and as men came home from the front the pressure for people to return to heteronormative gender roles mounted from many corners of society. In any case, Carson seemed powerless to keep saying no. She was in a new place, unable to write, unable to see well, months after losing her father to unspoken suicide. Carson writes in *Illumination*:

> I don't know why I felt I owed such devotion to him. Perhaps it was simply because he was the only man I had ever kissed, and the awful tyranny of pity. I knew he was not faithful to me sexually, but that did not matter to me, nor am I an especially maternal woman. . . . For some reason, certainly against my will, we became deeply involved with each other again and before I really knew what had happened, we were remarried.

In a history of Carson's outward-facing life, marriage hides a decade of manipulation and dysfunction, but by Carson's own account their second marriage was doomed from the start. Reeves got promoted to captain, took terminal leave, and moved to Nyack to live with Rita, Carson, and Bebe. Carson, meanwhile, headed to Yaddo for the summer of 1946 to finish *Wedding*.

# Dedications

Carson dedicated *The Member of the Wedding* to Elizabeth Ames. Elizabeth was the sole person she allowed to read the book in draft form, insisting that only she understood the feelings behind it.

# Fury and Disaster

Over the next four years, Carson finally published *The Member of the Wedding*, received her second Guggenheim Fellowship, met Tennessee Williams, learned to ski in Italy, had two more strokes, and attempted suicide. Tenn had written her a letter out of the blue in 1946 after staying up all night reading *Wedding*, and invited her to stay with him in Nantucket. Carson showed up in shorts and together they spent "a summer of sun and friendship" at the beach. "Every morning," she writes, "we would work at the same table, he at one end, and me at the other." She cooked Spuds Carson "almost every day," her own recipe which "consisted of baked potatoes, mashed with butter, onions, and cheese. After a long swim it was good fare." She befriended and later grew to despise Pancho Rodríguez, Tenn's partner, and told Tenn all about Reeves. Unexpectedly, Annemarie's old girlfriend, Baroness Margot Von Opel, stayed with them for some of the summer. Carson began a play version of *Member of the Wedding* in Nantucket, and Tenn helped her find a new agent, Audrey Wood.

Carson and Reeves traveled to Europe several times during these years, their last together, in various states of health and drunkenness. Lesbian writer and connector Janet Flanner welcomed Carson in Paris. Her partner, Natalia Murray, took Carson to her tailor in Rome and got her "the most beautiful pants suit she ever had in her entire life," which, sadly, didn't make it into the archive. Carson and Reeves were drinking heavily, noticeably on this trip, and Carson had her second stroke. She was treated at a hospital in Paris, where writer Richard Wright came to visit her and then leased her and Reeves his Paris apartment.

In a photo from one of her trips abroad, Carson and Reeves stand in the Piazza San Marco in Venice. Carson is smiling with her left arm tucked up, holding her cane. She is wearing the green tweed skirt suit that I catalogued. Her mouth is a fierce smile, but her eyes betray fear. Reeves stands about a foot and a half from her, holding a pigeon out at her, staring hard at the camera. He looks frightening. He has a boxer on a leash.

She writes in *Illumination* that during this trip, "Reeves's temper became more violent, and one night I felt his hands around my neck and I knew he was going to choke me. I bit him on his thumb with such violence that the blood spurted out and he let me go. The disappointment and the [dreadfulness] of those days might well have caused the last and final stroke from which I suffered." She had this final stroke alone in Paris in 1947, in Richard Wright and his wife's apartment, where she was staying apart from Reeves. When she was finally found on the floor of the apartment after eight hours and taken to the hospital, Wright chartered a plane to come see her. Reeves makes no appearance in Carson's retelling of this incident in *Illumination*. She and Reeves were then flown home from Europe ill: she weak from the fallout of her strokes, he with delirium tremens. I picture them laid out on stretchers on opposite sides of the plane.

# In Sickness

In the photo collection in Austin I found an image of Carson, washed out, grinning on an Adirondack chair. And then another of her in a V-neck sweater with her big collar and dark pants. The sweater looks like it's from the '70s but she didn't live that long—a fashion premonition—and on the back I find this piece of darkness: "Carson before stroke." Then another photo in a similar outfit but lighter, pleated pants and a collar tucked in, her posture less relaxed, her hands in fists, close to the house in Nyack, as though she couldn't walk very far. Her face is totally aged, drooping on one side. It's like she can't smile hard enough with her left side, but she's trying. "After stroke," the back of the photo does not say.

I struggle to comprehend the basic facts of Carson's illness and decline. I see the photos where her arm is in a splint, where her arm is hidden behind another person. I study the closest thing to a biography Mary Mercer ended up writing about Carson, a six-page handwritten timeline she titles

"Carson's Activities and Illnesses, 1936–1967." The first entries read, in their entirety:

> *1936 Met Reeves (Summer)*
> *1937 (Oct.) Married Reeves*
> *1940 (Summer) Divorced Reeves*
> *(Winter) 1st stroke*

The entry following their remarriage is from June 1947: "Sudden hemianopsia [blindness] and numbness Rt. hand. Impaired peripheral vision Rt. eye." Then in November, "Sudden, complete Left hemiplegia [paralysis]." My phone's search history includes "stroke" and "hemianopsia." I am trying to understand Carson the way I am trying to understand my own body: through research, diagnosis.

The people around Carson throughout her life each had their own interpretations of her illness, and those who weren't as close to her frequently questioned whether or not she was ever "really" sick. It is difficult to tell how much they knew of her medical history, to what extent Carson came out to others as a sick person. Boots writes, "Carson looks *very* well. She stays in bed a great deal of the time." These statements seem to contradict one another—if she's in bed all the time, doesn't she look sick? On learning that Carson had a double operation late in her life, Truman Capote informed Boots, "Well, I think Carson enjoys ill health." Boots replied, "There are people who enjoy the <u>results</u> of illness, but I have never known <u>anyone</u> who enjoyed illness."

Despite the best efforts of her interpreters, Carson speaks straightforwardly in her letters about how it feels to be in her body, and I take her at her word. "The last week was utter Hell," she writes to Tenn in 1949. She explains, "This last year has been unspeakably difficult. My health has failed steadily. I can't walk more than half a block, can't play the piano of course or type, can't smoke too much or, alas, get drunk. And neuritis has set in—the damaged nerves are constantly spastic and painful." She was thirty-two years old when she wrote that. She describes a three-day migraine, a gland in her neck that "went wrong" and "a sort of convulsion at dawn after the third day." In another letter, she tells Tenn that her pain and suffering would actually be humorous if it were happening to someone else. She isn't afraid of dying, she's afraid of another stroke. She writes, "The sinister illness that haunted my life all during my youth till the time I was twenty-nine had asserted itself. I lived in constant fear of strokes."

Carson, though she may not have always been the best caretaker of her body, struggled with her health from a very young age. Her first stroke, accompanied by partial paralysis and temporary blindness, happened the week before her twenty-fourth birthday, but it wasn't diagnosed as such for years. In a letter to Mary, she writes that she had been tortured by strokes, which she thought of then as strange fainting incidents, since her twenties, when she would find herself suddenly on the floor, unable to move, terrified. Each day she felt daunted by the possibility of damage to her brain. Some doctors told her she had a genetic brain malfunction, others believed her symptoms to be psychological. Without a satisfactory diagnosis, it was easiest to conclude that her sudden blindness, paralysis, and incapacitating migraines were all in her head.

When I started fainting, the doctors thought I was having seizures and began three months of testing on my brain to determine its condition. I was twenty-two, and I was told I could not drive at all, or climb stairs or ladders unattended. I had just started grad school and was teaching for the first time. Now, in addition to simply doubting my abilities, my intelligence, I was also made to question my brain and its basic functioning. Through months of scans and flashing lights I lived in constant paranoia, uncertain about the reliability of my own thoughts. The fullest diagnosis of what was actually a heart condition (hypovolemia and postural orthostatic tachycardia syndrome, or POTS) came a few years later, as I was beginning to research Carson.

To question, to cast doubt, on how a person experiences her own body is cruel and damaging, and all too common. Carson was misdiagnosed several times, starting with the rheumatic fever at eighteen that would eventually cause her

strokes, which her doctor treated at the time as tuberculosis. Even her strokes were explained to her as psychological
episodes, triggered by emotional trauma. The psychologiz-
ing of illness complicates the relationship between self and
body. Susan Sontag points out that, on the one hand, to
psychologize illness is to view "every form of social devia-
tion" as illness: from criminal behavior to addiction to, say,
homosexuality. But at the same time, if any malady can
be connected to a patient's psychology, it follows that on
some conscious or unconscious level people can get sick on
purpose, and if they really wanted to be well, they could
cure themselves. Certainly this is how many people choose
to interpret others' addictions, and even their own: as bad
habits. This double bind instills a pervasive sense that illness is not real, that what the self experiences is not valid.
The chronically ill person, thus: the "invalid."

The confusion of these years indicates that Carson was
drinking far more than she should have been, and it also
suggests memory failures, a likely outcome of strokes and
possibly a consequence of trauma. Carson spent much of
1948 ill at home in Nyack, after separating again from
Reeves. In March, she ended up in Payne Whitney Psychiatric Clinic after slashing her left wrist. She told Dr. William Mayer, a psychiatrist she was confiding in during this
period, that she and Reeves were separated, their second
marriage only a formality. She stopped writing regularly to
Tenn for a while, but soon he heard from Janet Flanner that

Carson was not well. He came up with a plan for Carson to move out West with him, to a ranch in Mexico, where, he wrote, they could take care of his sister and work in "adjoining trances" as they had in Nantucket. Instead, Carson and Reeves reconciled again. Another form of self-destruction: choosing the person who harms you.

# Witch Hunt

Carson planned a trip south with Bebe, to visit Boots and his partner, Paul Bigelow, in Macon, and Edwin and John in Charleston. On this trip, Carson was called suddenly to return to New York and offer assistance to Ames, who found herself under fire from a group of Yaddo writers for alleged communist sympathies. The war years had provided a degree of freedom for public queer expression, as bars and queer communities like February House brought people together and provided access to larger networks of queer people. In the years that followed, this freedom proved to be a resource for those seeking to prove a person's "perversion" in the climate of McCarthyism. The Kinsey Reports, published in two installments in 1948 and 1953, indicated just how widespread and omnipresent gay people were, and government officials began to elide communist sympathies with queerness. Anyone with a secret identity must be a spy, and anyone with deviant inclinations must be removed from their jobs. The FBI granted ordinary citizens new license to monitor the behavior of their friends and neighbors in the interest of national security under the purview of the Red Scare and the Lavender Scare that grew alongside it.

After providing a queer and political haven for its artists for many years, Yaddo was in for a scandal, what came to be called the "Lowell Affair." In early February 1949, allegations of communist sympathies came out in the papers against a lesbian journalist named Agnes Smedley, who had been in residence at Yaddo for five years. In 1948, Ames had asked Smedley, who was rumored to be a communist, to leave Yaddo for fear of the consequences of her associations, but it was too late. Yaddo secretary Emma Townsend had been secretly informing the FBI for two years about "any guests who made what she considered disloyal remarks" during their stays, writes Ruth Price in *Yaddo: Making American Culture.* Without any proof against Smedley, the FBI showed up at Yaddo and began questioning residents and staff. One resident left the colony immediately. Four others took up arms against Ames for playing "a leading and fully conscious role" in a "dangerous communist conspiracy" at Yaddo. Freshly Catholic and bipolar poet Robert Lowell, along with his soon-to-be wife, writer Elizabeth Hardwick, twenty-four-year-old Flannery O'Connor, and writer Edward Maisel held a makeshift trial in one of Yaddo's garages, questioning Ames and others about their involvement with Smedley.

When they mentioned "involvement" with Smedley, though no one said this aloud, they meant *romantic* involvement. Smedley had stayed at Yaddo for several years to help Ames care for her ailing sister, Marjorie. Lowell et al. wanted Ames fired on the spot because she "was somehow deeply and mysteriously connected" with Smedley's "political activities." They considered her "totally unfitted for the position of executive director." The word "unfitted" here is important. Joseph McCarthy made it clear in his Red Scare speeches not only that homosexuality was a kind of sociopathy but also that queer people were more likely to be swayed by communist ideas because of their "peculiar mental twists." Smedley had been accused of, among other things, perverting young women at neighboring Skidmore College. To question Ames's fitness for her job because of her connection to Smedley was to question her sexual orientation and, essentially, insist that Yaddo could not have a queer woman at its helm. Lowell was gunning for the directorship at Yaddo, according to several artists in residence at the time. If Ames was not fired immediately for her deep, mysterious involvement with Smedley, Lowell vowed to "blacken the name of Yaddo as widely as possible," using his connections in the literary sphere and in Washington to do so.

By several accounts, Lowell's behavior at Yaddo in 1949 and in the ensuing years was manic; it eventually landed him in a McLean Hospital. Lowell had a vision of Ames and her crimes and prayed that she might be "purged" of her "pollution." He had another vision of O'Connor anointed as a saint. Lowell's only written recollections of those months come from his time in Indiana before his institutionalization: "Seven years ago I had an attack of pathological enthusiasm. The night before I was locked up I ran about the streets of Bloomington Indiana crying out against devils and homosexuals."

Carson was one of many writers and artists who came out in support of Elizabeth with letters and a petition signed by fifty-five of their number, which described "very grave political accusations that were arrived at overnight, and hurled at Mrs. Ames in an atmosphere strangely comparable to that of a purge trial," with no evidence but Lowell's visions and what Hardwick referred to as her "intuition." When she heard the news, Carson and her mother boarded a train from Macon back to New York, where Carson hoped to be of assistance to her friend, but by the time she arrived the crisis had been resolved. The Yaddo board of directors met in March and dropped all charges against Elizabeth, who remained the director until 1969. However, a certain amount of psychological damage had been done, and Elizabeth was hospitalized after the scandal. The following year, the McCarthy trials began.

When I find myself hoping for a Carson more willing to be open about her sexuality, when I wish that Carson would just come out already in a way that is more obvious and recognizable and in print, I think of Robert Lowell. And when I think of Robert Lowell, I always think of Eileen Myles's poem "On the Death of Robert Lowell," which ends,

Take Robert Lowell.
The old white-haired coot.
Fucking dead.

# This Mad Desire for Travel

In her thirties, Carson spent more and more time staying with her friends and avoiding Reeves, perhaps earning her the reputation as burdensome, needy, to some. She continued to write to Elizabeth and to work on the edits she got from Tenn for the play of *The Member of the Wedding*. It opened on Broadway to huge acclaim in January 1950, though Carson refused as always to attend the opening. She wasn't feeling well that week and went to the doctor for some tests, where she learned she was pregnant. In *Illumination*, she writes that when Bebe found out about her condition, she told the doctor, who viewed the pregnancy as a blessing, that she'd "do something about it," meaning an abortion: "You don't know what it is to have a baby. It will kill my child." Bebe was familiar with her daughter's ongoing illness and so was deeply protective of her. She knew that, after three strokes, Carson couldn't handle a pregnancy. Not to mention that Carson was drinking heavily. The doctor, according to Carson, still encouraged her to have the baby, but her mother intervened. Dr. Mayer,

Carson's psychiatrist at the time, was equally worried and made arrangements for her to terminate the pregnancy.

When Carson narrates her pregnancy in *Illumination*, she does not mention telling Reeves or include him in recounting the doctor's visit or the decision-making process. Frankly, it's not clear who the father is. Carson states that she was so upset by her mother's argument with the doctor, she miscarried that weekend. "The miscarriage was not easy," she writes. She stayed home all weekend, Bebe refusing to call a doctor out of "some outlandish fear that either they might put the baby back or do something that would kill me in the end." On Monday, Carson bled all over the taxi on the way to the hospital, where the chief gynecologist asked Reeves, "Why have you waited till now? Your wife is dying." The doctor immediately started transfusions.

In *The Lonely Hunter*, Carr suggests that Carson actually had an abortion, which would mean the anecdote in her autobiography is at least partially fabricated. If that is the case, perhaps she didn't feel she could include the fact of an abortion in print, though she makes it clear that Bebe was outright demanding one. Savigneau states that Carson never wanted children, though I have yet to find confirmation of this in her own words. When she found out she was pregnant, Carson writes, she was "surprised but pleased." However, in her narration she doesn't mention whether she wanted to have the child, or wanted an abortion, or even whether she was upset about the miscarriage. She lets Bebe's and the doctor's opinions and voices shape the narrative.

By the spring of 1950, she was well enough to travel to Ireland to visit Elizabeth Bowen, who later referred to her as "'a terrible handful'" of a houseguest: Carson mistook the time difference and called in the middle of the night before her arrival, got bored with the quiet of the house and interrupted Bowen's work, and generally just milled around until the evening, when guests arrived and drinks were served by what Carson called the "public fireplace," where she could finally feel at home telling stories to anyone who would listen, and causing mild uproar. For her part, Carson enjoyed her stay, and in *Illumination* she recalls the "little floating duck" in the bathtub she used there. She met up with Reeves in Paris, and inevitably they separated again. Back in New York, Reeves took his own apartment and Carson went to stay on Fire Island with lesbian couple Marty Mann and Priscilla Peck, who had tried to get Reeves into a twelve-step program.

Fire Island was already an active community for queer people (those who could afford it—mostly white, middle-class designers, cultural producers, and members of the theater world) when Carson came to visit. She was well known in Cherry Grove, the town at the center of the queer community on the island. One skit in the 1948 Cherry Grove Follies was called "Dismembering the Wedding," "a send-up of *Member of the Wedding*," in which "a butch-looking woman played the housekeeper Bernice Brown in a gingham apron and an eye-patch, a 'girl' played the tomboy Frankie Adams in loafers and socks topped by a silver lamé dress and chiffon scarves, and a barelegged 'boy' played the young John Henry West in a T-shirt and tutu." Visitors to Fire Island in the 1950s tended to conceal the place from their straight friends in the city, saying they'd spent the weekend on Long Island or in Southampton. In therapy with Mary, Carson describes the conundrum of a male friend of hers who is pining after a woman who has gone away for the weekend with another woman. Carson casually mentions to Mary that the two women shared a room on Fire Island, a telling shorthand for their relationship.

When Tennessee Williams threw a party for the British writer Edith Sitwell in New York, Carson, meeting the writer for the first time, sat with Edith on the sofa and the two talked about their work all night. Carson mailed her copies of her novels, and after reading them, Edith invited her to visit her house in England. In the Ransom Center's reading room, a squadron of marble busts of writers whose papers are housed in the archive perches on the shelves lining the periphery. Sitwell's is the only bust in the room of a female writer.

Carson continued to spend much of the year apart from Reeves, separated officially or effectively. While her marriage was an ongoing struggle for autonomy and, more than perhaps anything else, peace, her career had never been more solid. The movie rights to *Wedding* were purchased in 1951. With the money, Carson bought Bebe a house at 131 South Broadway in South Nyack, the house in which Carson would live for the rest of her life.

Separated from Reeves, Carson decided to sail alone to England to visit her new friend, Edith. Aboard the *Queen Elizabeth*, as Carson recalls to Mary in therapy in 1958, she saw a man who looked exactly like Reeves. She saw him several times, at a distance. Then one day, she received a letter from Reeves "saying that he was on the boat, and that he was going to jump overboard unless I would reconcile with him." It is hard to identify the beginning of the end of their relationship, given how difficult it was from the start, given Carson's "ambivalence" going all the way back to the porch on Stark Avenue. During this period, Carson explains, "these threats and emotional blackmail became a daily pattern. If I wouldn't take him back he would kill himself; the same refrain. I was hesitant to give a curt and truthful answer. I was always so afraid he would actually fulfill his threats, which in the end he did." (After one of his attempts at hanging himself, a biographer writes, Carson "reportedly admonished him: 'Please, Reeves, if you *must* commit suicide, do it somewhere else. Just look what you did to my favorite pear tree.'") When she arrived in England, Carson sent Reeves back home. He returned to Nyack and lived with Bebe, while Carson stayed in England for three months visiting friends.

# Going West

In the fall of 1951, back in Nyack with Reeves and Bebe, Carson began a piece about a pharmacist called "The Pestle," the seeds for her final novel, *Clock Without Hands*, which she would publish ten years later. She and Reeves sailed one last time for Europe, to Naples and then Rome, and finally to a home outside Paris, "a small house, but Reeves and I had separate bedrooms and there was a guest room." Reeves was drinking constantly in the cellar beneath his "studio," where he claimed to be writing a book, and he was continuing to threaten Carson. He had his sights set on a double suicide, convinced that they could never be happy, together or apart, and the only solution was to die as a couple. I read this as his acceptance of Carson's love for women and his own unspeakable love for men, that because they are queer they can never love each other completely, though it's impossible to know what he was thinking. (He had proposed the same solution, joint suicide, to David Diamond once, going so far as to push him toward the edge of a bridge.) In late summer, 1953, Reeves drove

Carson into the woods. At her feet, on the floor of the passenger side, Carson saw the ropes. They stopped at a gas station and while Reeves was inside, Carson fled the car, fled Reeves, fled France. This time, thank god, for good.

I remember feeling horrified when I first read this in one of Carson's biographies. She doesn't describe the scene in *Illumination*, but she refers to Reeves as a potential murderer multiple times. To me it shows how far manipulation and possessiveness can go in a relationship. Silence and secrecy around queer desires—Reeves's refusal to accept his own sexuality, Carson's "imaginary friends"—can create a desperation that leads to extreme beliefs about a single relationship's importance and ability to define a person's whole identity, whole world. I'm furious that Carson stayed with Reeves this long, but I also think I understand how hard it was to see a way out when so much was governed by Reeves's increasing delusions and manipulations.

In Paris, Janet Flanner continued to care for and support Reeves in Carson's absence. According to her biographer, Janet had "always been sensitive to the myriad of causes underlying Reeves's unhappiness and empathized with his suffering and confusion, his uncertainty about who he was and what he should be doing." She told Carson, "We all recognized ourselves in Reeves. Each of us recognized the 'disorientation' we have all fought against." Reeves in turn saw Janet as among the last people in the world who cared for him. He once asked David, "Do you think she will come to close my eyes when I die?" Back in the US, Carson learned that Reeves had killed himself in a hotel in Paris in November after sending cryptic messages to everyone he knew in town informing them he was "going West." To Janet, he sent what she called "the most beautiful flowers I ever received in my life."

Carson refused to pay to have Reeves's body returned to the US and did not attend his funeral abroad, asking Janet to go in her place. Many people were quick to criticize Carson for what seemed like callousness. None of the newspapers printed Reeves's cause of death, mentioning an automobile accident or "natural causes." Very few knew what had happened between them, in France or throughout their relationship, but plenty of people came to see Carson as coldhearted. Reeves's family broke off all contact with her.

Carson struggled to discuss Reeves in her conversations with Mary. She writes, "Mary understood. She did not think it was romantic when he sneaked onto the Queen Mary [*sic*] and threatened to jump overboard if I wouldn't take him back. She sensed, as I knew, that we were dealing with a potential murderer as well as a thoroughly dishonest man." Here (as though I am the authority on this matter) I have to credit Mary with knowing Carson better than her biographers, better than so many of the people around her. Like Elizabeth, she understood that Reeves was a great threat to Carson's independence, her work, and her sense of self—as well as her life. This was no great romance, no life-long love. Maybe what they had could be described as love, but I have trouble recognizing it as something other than pursuit and possession at all costs. Reeves was a shadow that loomed over Carson's whole adult life, one with which she continuously reckoned but was never able to shake while he was alive. When he was finally gone, I can only imagine her feeling of relief. Freedom.

Carson writes to Mary in 1958 that since falling in love with her, her pressing wanderlust has quite subsided.

# Coping Mechanisms

When she went to Yaddo for the last time in the summer of 1954, at thirty-seven, crawling her way back from the traumas of the previous year, Carson finished a draft of *The Square Root of Wonderful*, a new play, while Elizabeth and Rita exchanged letters about Carson's drinking. Carson was staying in Pine Garde, Elizabeth's residence at Yaddo, a building where I did my laundry in a basement that felt truly haunted. Elizabeth insisted that Rita—who had joined AA—not repeat anything about Carson's visits with a local doctor or their discussions of her alcoholism. Bebe, an alcoholic herself, wrote frequently to Boots, to Bigelow, and to Tenn about Carson's health and drinking.

Carson went to visit Tenn in Key West in the spring of 1955, where she worked on a stage adaptation of *Ballad*, a short story version of *Square Root*, and her new novel, *Clock Without Hands*, while Tenn wrote to deadline on the revised version of *Cat on a Hot Tin Roof.* In June, a few weeks after Carson returned to New York, Bebe died of a heart attack.

She was sixty-five, and Ida Reeder, the nurse who would later care for Carson, was the only person with her in the house in Nyack. Carson was staying with friends in the city, and when she heard the news from Boots that her mother had died, "it was too much, almost too much." She didn't want to come home and face the fact of her mother's body. "I had slept with my mother in twin beds for all the years that she had been delicate," she writes in *Illumination*. After the funeral, to which Carson wore all white, everyone stayed up drinking and toasting Bebe, who had been a constant presence among Carson and her friends. Bebe had been drinking sherry to the end and suffered from bleeding ulcers. It seems that Carson and Bebe enabled each other to drink, while each tried to watch out for and take care of the other.

So many people in Carson's life talked to each other about her drinking, but I wonder if anyone talked to Carson about it. In *Illumination*, Carson mentions alcoholism—her maternal grandfather's, Reeves's ("he had a splendid constitution and I would not have recognized alcoholism in those days") but not her own or her mother's. Carson set limits on her drinking and described attempts to cut back in her letters to Reeves during the war, and in her conversations with Mary, but her words suggest that she saw it more as a bad habit than as an unbeatable addiction.

Carson, Tenn, and Reeves (and Annemarie, David, Boots, Janet, all the others) lived through an era of hatred and persecution of homosexuality that lasted throughout the twentieth century but was worst in the 1930s and again in the '50s, with the slight reprieve of the war years, and each of them struggled with their sexual identities in their own way. It is not hard to draw the line between being unable to care for yourself, drinking yourself ill, and queer self-hatred. There is a tendency to blame the ill for their illness: to seek out a person's bad decisions, their unhealthy behaviors, and point to these as proof of a personal failure instead of offering help or sympathy. In each of her biographies, Carson's drinking hovers under the surface, never adequately addressed, but always mentioned in the context of her illness. When her contemporaries recall her, she usually has a drink in hand. To what extent her drinking contributed to her illness, to her weakness, cannot be determined. I'm not all that sure that parsing this connectedness matters. Sick is sick.

Tennessee understood this. He wrote Carson:

> *I am a vulnerable person, but it frightens me to see how even <u>more</u> vulnerable <u>you</u> are. Is there no way you can defend and spare yourself, learn how to live not so acutely, and still be yourself and an artist? I have been so careful of myself physically because I have to—to live—but you are quite heedless about keeping yourself physically well. When you get up again you must promise all who love you to treat yourself with all the*

*tenderness and wisdom that your work deserves from you. Think only of restoration.*

What Tenn calls her vulnerability, her living "acutely," transcends the physical body and includes it. When I read these words, I associate them with anxiety, with my own anxiety, which feels to me like an oversensitivity to the world around me. I am lucky to live at a moment when there are many non-life-threatening options for managing anxiety—Lexapro and meditation and exercise help enormously to make it possible for me to live with my own brain. But for Carson, for Tenn, for Reeves, whom Tenn describes in a letter to Bigelow as "a very sick person and a very pitifully maladjusted one," and for so many writers, especially queer writers, at midcentury, anxiety was the reality and drinking or pills the only way to soothe it. How else would someone with a secret, criminalized, pathologized identity feel but anxious and depressed?

In the 1950s, queerness was still understood as a congenital disorder. Up until the nineteenth century, sexual "deviance" was seen as a sinful behavior, but when Western medicine got involved, it became a symptom of a faulty body, a degenerate self. Medical or psychiatric treatment was the solution to this "problem." Though it isn't said outright in any of the biographies, Annemarie's hospitalizations, insulin shock treatment, and the choice she was given between institutionalization and deportation likely sought to cure her "diseased" inclinations toward women as much as to treat her morphine addiction. During these same years, Alan Turing was persecuted and Carl Solomon was institutionalized (voluntarily) at what Allen Ginsberg calls "Rockland" in *Howl.* Is it any wonder that Carson was averse to visiting a therapist? Lesbians in the 1940s and '50s would go to therapy for insomnia or anxiety and be met with sexual conversion therapy. Pulp lesbian novels circulated, but could pass through the censors only if the protagonist chose a man in the end or was killed. Often she killed herself. The main cultural representations of women who loved women depicted them as tortured, sick, and unfit for living. Queerness can still be construed as a similar kind of weakness of will, an unfitness to live a normal life or to meet social expectations.

My own chronic illness connects to fear, the feeling of not being real that accompanies queer womanhood. I don't always remember or believe my illness is real, because there is no reflection of it outside myself, my own feelings. As a "fashionable illness," it is a subject of ridicule (like Carson's "obsessions" with women) or something that others fail or refuse to acknowledge (like lesbian invisibility).

# Seismographs

Society tends to be suspicious of sick people, probably because we cannot feel precisely what a sick person feels. As a chronically ill person, on bad days I am aware that my body is in pain but no one can see it. I look the same. To think or talk about being sick makes me feel unduly self-pitying, or self-aggrandizing, or self-obsessed. I once heard Maggie Nelson describe the self as a seismograph for experiences: senses, feelings, and thoughts are facts only the self knows. When I am a body in pain, I have only self to turn to. Even well-meaning others can't see or know or feel the facticity of all my skin aching at a light draft. For this same reason, it is difficult to chart the illness of a historical figure in relation to illness today. Illness is both culturally constructed and subjective. It is both within and without, felt in our bodies but filtered by the faulty language we have been given to describe it.

Carson wrote each of her books during a bout of illness, bed rest, or recovery, including her first novel. Rest is often considered to be a failure—failure to be productive, to function—and exhaustion is not a quality that the world takes very seriously, at least not the worlds I have inhabited. Energy is the prized possession of the young and the deepest desire of the aging. In her later years, Carson was in bed by ten. "I want to be able to write whether in sickness or in health," she writes, "for indeed, my health depends almost completely on my writing."

I often feel bedridden and work from bed. It's hard to write on the days when I can't sit up. Sometimes I just feel bad, weak, foggy. Illness is lonely and frequently hard. I'm left with my own ongoing wondering if this sense of loneliness is just me or if it's a human feeling. I think this is one thing that drew me to Carson's fiction in the first place. On the page, Carson is at pains to articulate the inarticulable, to find a way to express feelings of isolation, loneliness, and longing that I associate with queer life, with life as a sick person, and with life as a writer.

I get a lot of sleep, I try not to drink too much, I eat well, I go on long walks for my weak heart, but I am still a queer, sick, writing person—woman—living in the world. I get lonely. I am alone because I don't have the energy to participate as much as I'd like to, I'm alone because writing demands that I be alone, and I feel lonely because the world that finds its way through to me, via the internet, or invitations I often turn down, or cancelled plans, suggests that life is happening elsewhere. It is someplace outside my home, where I work, and outside my mind, where I often live. It can be lonely to be queer, especially if you choose to forego the usual signposts of a complete life, like marriage and children. And it is lonely to be a writer, to put your work first and your income second in a world that would rather you find a full-time job and earn more money. To stay home, to be sick, to write can make all of my life feel like a place out of time. In Austin, in my twenties, when I needed to remember that the world was still there, that I was still in it, I used to sit out on the porch smoking cigarettes, staring into the middle distance, wondering what my neighbor was doing. In my new, quieter life in New Mexico, I walk outside several times a day to babysit the puny vegetables, or look out at the mountains over our adobe walls.

# Diagnosis

I saw a new therapist in Santa Fe and she gave me a civilian PTSD checklist to fill out. I looked down at the questions and tried to stay present in the room until the end of the session, but already as I left the building I was applying the diagnosis to Carson. I was asking her these questions: Have you ever had "1. Repeated, disturbing *memories, thoughts* or *images* of a stressful experience from the past? 2. Repeated, disturbing *dreams* of a stressful experience from the past? . . . 6. Avoid[ed] *thinking about* or *talking about* a stressful experience from the past or avoided *having feelings* related to it?" Yes, yes, and yes, I answered for her. Her life was a cascade of trauma, much of it undiscussed until her sessions with Mary: Annemarie, Reeves, her father, her strokes and the ensuing paralysis, temporary blindness, not to mention the trauma of being queer without the language or space to express it. It wasn't until the last years of her life that things calmed down enough for her even to try to tell her side of the story.

Those who were close to Carson encouraged her to be careful, to take care of herself. As when Elizabeth wrote to her, "I hope all that you have had to bear will not wear you down too much. Your gifts are great; think of yourself as their guardian and let nothing play havoc with them." Or Annemarie: "Dear Darling, I know stronger than ever. That, in order to be true to our work, we must be brave and face lonelyness [*sic*]. I know you learned a lot about it since you were so terribly ill—but I want you to be strong enough, oh Carson,—to stand even your weak health: it is, combined with your beautiful and pure talent, your great chance." Or Mary's constant refrain when they were apart, "Go gently, gently."

# Blue Chair

I did not sit in Carson's blue chair. I did not even take a picture of it. There are two pale blue armchairs in the room of the Stark Avenue house I called the "entertainment room"—a record player, a mounted flat-screen TV, a piano, and the organ—but I could tell from photos which chair was the favorite, the one Carson could sit comfortably in right up to the end. I didn't touch that chair. Several newspaper articles refer to Carson as "wheelchair bound" in the 1950s and '60s, but I've seen only a few photos of her in a wheelchair. If true, this implies that someone— Ida, Mary—would lift her in their arms and place her in the blue chair. A beautiful image of care. Illness as revelator of love. As the photos flip back in time from folder to folder, Carson looks frail and small in the chair, then she looks spry and sprawling in a shawl with a friend, a Japanese painter, then there is a photo of her nurse, Ida, in the chair after Carson is gone. When I think of my time in Columbus my imagination will often first conjure this room, where I sat on the couch in the evenings watching

Hillary win the presidential primary and episodes of *Buffy*, on the phone with Chelsea doing the same. Where the chair should be, there is a gap in my memory, a smudge on the lens.

# Organ

I tried several times to play it, but couldn't get it to sound. The organ stands in the corner of the entertainment room, taller than I am and dark wood and ornately carved. It was a gift from Carson to Mary Mercer.

The last day of my stay at the house, the director of the McCullers Center sat me down in a coffee shop with Bible verses decorating each table to tell me he had heard in no uncertain terms that Carson and Mary were "never romantically involved." I'm wondering what that even means, "romantically involved," because what else can we call it that Mary saved every single letter, postcard, telegram, and valentine that Carson wrote her during the nine years they spent together? Not to mention every tiny card that came stuck in a bouquet of flowers Carson sent her, at least fifty of which I dutifully scanned for my files. When Carson died, Rita tried to sell her house in Nyack and all it contained, but Mary, after a series of fraught letters, bought it and kept it exactly as it had been, even the gardens. These commodities, these records of consumer goods exchanged, this real estate are all that linger, all that we can point to and say "love." The Stark Avenue house is full of Carson's wedding photos, but the organ looms.

# Last Love

Carson fell in love with Mary when she was forty-one. In *Illumination* she describes her "meeting with and love for Dr. Mary" as "the happiest and most rewarding experiences of my life." Carson does not come out about their relationship any further in the book; her letters to Mary tell more. After Mary had discharged her as a patient in 1958, Carson wrote to her that she had illuminated her life, and that this light would continue to shine for the entire time that Carson went on loving her. She could imagine nothing that might take away from this illumination.

When Mary traveled abroad, that summer after their therapy sessions concluded, she gave Carson her ring to keep her company. Carson wrote to her that she almost cried when she left, but the sight of Mary's ring consoled her. She thanked Mary for allowing her to hold on to a piece of her while she was away. Mary replied in a handwritten draft that she saved, "It pleases me that that ring has been of comfort. It has done the same for me too in its time: its color, smoothness, weight and symmetry." Her letter, an unsent draft, is the only example of her writing to Carson that she kept. It is riddled with revisions that I decide to read as signs of editorial affection. Why else would she need to get so exactly right her descriptions of the sea, of swimming, which she crossed out and rewrote in the margins?

She tells Carson that she has "found a copy of *Love in the Western World* to take with me. I have read it carefully, thoughtfully. It may save us much time and I cannot thank you enough for putting it into my hands." *Love in the Western World*, a comparative history of romantic love, suggests that while certain kinds of self-destructive passion are often celebrated in the pages of Western literature, love in its ideal form allows for a separateness of the beloved, rather than an annihilation of the self. The author, Denis de Rougemont, had visited February House back in the 1940s. It is unclear how and why this book became so important to Carson and Mary, how it would save them time. But it makes room for many different types and interpretations of love.

When Carson died, Mary insisted that she be buried "wearing the silver and turquoise ring she had given her, which Carson wore constantly."

# Not Yet

Last year I took a dumb online quiz while friends were in town—we all took it—and learned that gifts are my "love language," so it is possible that I imbue objects exchanged with more significance than others might. I read Carson and Mary's love through these objects, and I realize that I do the same with mine and Chelsea's. I think not of rings but of the amethyst pendant she gave me for my thirtieth birthday. When our friends in Santa Fe see it they ask if I ever use it as a pendulum for making decisions. I tell them not yet. I think of the blue Mexican blanket we took on our first picnic, to the golf course, where we fucked and talked for hours in the dark and got chased away by the sprinklers. The next day she texted that she hadn't shaken the grass off the blanket, couldn't bring herself to do it. I wrote back, *Of course not. It's our grass.* It's the blanket we cover the couch with at night now, in our loft in Santa Fe.

It isn't easy to narrate happiness or love, and it's hard to prove their existence through recorded facts and descriptions.

What is the precise evidence for love? Documentation of sexual encounters? Examples of daily intimacies? Easier to tell and to corroborate are stories of pain, dramatic events, betrayals. Love meanwhile lives in the mundane, the moment-to-moment exchanges, and can so easily become invisible after the people who shared it are no longer alive. But, of course, it leaves traces.

# First Loves

Carson was in love with two Marys, Mary Tucker, her piano teacher, at the beginning of her life, and Mary Mercer, her therapist, at the end. After Carson died, the Marys started writing to each other about her. Most of this correspondence has been lost; these were the letters Mary Mercer asked be destroyed. Carson's devotion to Mary Tucker was among the first of her inarticulable loves. She told Mary Mercer that everything she had loved had been untouchable, and that she couldn't speak up about her feelings. Mary Tucker she thought of as superhuman, and couldn't even bear to hug her. She was able to express how she felt only through music. Prior to Mary Mercer, Carson couldn't pursue any kind of psychiatric help because she wasn't able to share her story, in the same way, she suggests, that she wasn't free to express her feelings for Mary Tucker. In July 1958, Carson writes to Mary Mercer of her desire for self-discipline, promising that she will cut back on her drinking. She then tells Mary that what she feels for her is as gentle and abiding as the love she once felt for Mary

Tucker, and that, like her childhood love, this feeling could be generative and productive for her writing.

On the porch with Reeves, when he asked if she was a lesbian, Carson said that she had loved Mary Tucker and Vera, a family friend, but hadn't told them. She had always kept them at some remove. Unable to share her feelings physically or in words, Carson found other ways to show her love. Mary Tucker taught her to express her feelings through music; her creative outlet was also the outlet for her desire. In therapy, Carson explains how she communicated her love to Vera: fudge. While Vera was at Hollins College, and Carson was wildly in love with her, she made her fudge and sent it to her, one batch after the next, so that Vera had a supply the whole time she was in school. When Carson says she was in love, I believe she means she was in love.

# Dream

After their first therapy session, Carson wrote a letter to Mary telling her about two dreams. In one, she is struggling to get her coat on and Mary offers her oyster stew. *Oyster stew*, lesbian readers! In the other, a doctor named Monique, who Carson knew in Paris appears, and Carson can't reach her because things get in her way, causing her to despair. The dream shifts, and Carson is suddenly in the Alps. The image she conjures next, knowing that she arrived at Mary's for their first session walking with a cane and couldn't open the door due to partial paralysis, is fairly outrageous: in her dream, Carson is skiing. She alludes to Switzerland, recalling Annemarie's homeland, and tells Mary parenthetically that Switzerland has for a long time had a great significance to her. In the dream, she feels tranquil, exultant. She tells Mary that she thinks Monique represents her, and that, by skiing together, she imagines that Mary can set her free.

Carson links a woman from her past with feeling comfortable in her body. Monique taught her to ski in the '40s, before her last strokes rendered her left side permanently paralyzed, and in this dream skiing is freedom: from queer obstacles, from despair. With Mary, and to Mary, Carson imagines a body unimpeded by the paralysis and weakness of her later years, a heart calmed.

The next letter in the file, written two months later, begins with Carson declaring to Mary her sense of awe at their unexpected new love.

# Matters of Taste

After reading over the transcripts of their therapy and informing Mary that it was all garbage, Carson started to type again, with one hand. The letters she wrote to Mary, the narrations of her dreams, these were the beginning of her return to writing.

Carson's life in the late 1950s and early '60s, and her writings from these years—a play, a novel, and a book of children's poems—tend to be ignored or forgotten. Carlos Dews writes that "the final fifteen years of McCullers's life saw a marked decline in her health and creative output." Writer's block is one of the themes of *Illumination*, and Carson describes "so many frightful times when I was 'un-illuminated,' and feared that I could never write again. This fear is one of the horrors of an author's life. Where does work come from? What chance, what small episode will start the chain of creation?" In this case, Mary—or the revelations born of their conversations and ensuing partnership—is the spark that gets her writing when she thought she was stuck forever. In a letter to Mary early on in their therapy, she writes that her novel has drawn near to her at last, that she is overjoyed to have it close again.

A few weeks after their therapy concluded, Carson returned to the manuscript she had started ten years before. With Mary's help, she learned that she could have operations on her hand to make it more functional, which she did. She began to write again. After working on her last novel for the better part of a decade, Carson finished *Clock Without Hands* within a year of her sessions with Mary.

*Clock Without Hands*, published in 1961, brings together Carson's own experience with illness and decline, the racist and homophobic attitudes of small southern communities, and the first rumblings of the civil rights movement and white backlash: the bombings of homes purchased by black people in neighborhoods deemed "white" by the KKK. Of all McCullers's fiction, this novel speaks most directly to our own moment. It documents the 1960s prominence of the KKK, the resentful persecution of blacks and queers, and a belief held by conservative white southerners in the unqualified rightness of their power and wealth. Flannery O'Connor "said that it was absolutely the worst book she had ever read," according to Carr. Boots's father, a judge on whom Carson based one of the characters, hated it so much he threw the book across the room when he finished reading it. According to Boots, "Daddy also objected to 'those things in the book that a woman just ought not to be writing about.'. . . . In that, he may seem to be the product of his generation and religious upbringing, but to him this is a matter of taste, not of morality."

*Clock* has an openly gay character, and another, Jester, who is trying to understand his love for another man. Jester asks his grandfather, the conservative judge, "Have you ever read the Kinsey Report?" The reference suggests Carson's own piqued interest in its findings on human sexuality. She includes a joke for the reader familiar with the report: "The old Judge had read the book with salacious pleasure, first substituting for the jacket the dust cover of *The Decline and Fall of the Roman Empire.*" He tells his gay grandson that the landmark study he read clandestinely is "just tomfoolery and filth."

The year *Clock* was published, Mary quietly divorced her husband, Ray. Carson and Mary traveled together to visit friends—Edwin and John in Charleston, Mary Tucker in Virginia, and Edward Albee on Fire Island, where he and Carson worked on a stage production of *The Ballad of the Sad Café.* Albee wrote each morning for four hours, then, at night, returning from walking the beach, he read aloud to Carson and Mary. He read Samuel Beckett's *Happy Days* and his own *Who's Afraid of Virginia Woolf?* and the first act of *Ballad.* One of the major obstacles to staging *Ballad* was the question of Amelia's motivations. Albee asked Carson for an explanation: "'What went on upstairs when Marvin Macy tried to get in bed with Miss Amelia? Was Miss Amelia a lesbian?'" According to Albee, Carson wanted this left ambiguous.

Carson held a now-famous lunch for Marilyn Monroe, Arthur Miller, and Karen Blixen (pen name Isak Dinesen), a friend to whom she'd been writing for years, at her house in Nyack. She served oysters and champagne, the only things Blixen would eat at the time. Writing to Mary, who was traveling during the festivities, she says how she missed her at the party, that it was a day they would have relived together in their golden years. When Carson traveled, Mary came to meet her at the airport, the contemporary definition of love.

I have yet to encounter another person who has read *Clock Without Hands* except at my urging, though when it came out it was a best seller. For the author photo, Carson had to sit in a high-backed chair because she could not hold her head up on her own. Perhaps it comes down to matters of taste whether we are interested in the later years of a woman writer's life, whether we are interested in what she has to say when she is bedridden and wheelchair-bound, when she has to take heartburn medication to cope with the stress of a book deal. She was forty-four when the book came out and would not make it past fifty.

# Dedications

Carson dedicated *Clock Without Hands* "For Mary E. Mercer, M.D."

# Dream

At the end of June 1958, four months after their first meeting, Carson began a letter to Mary with another dream. In the dream, she has her arms wrapped around Mary, hugging and kissing her, but Mary's spirit feels far away and Carson doesn't know how to express her love. Dream Carson reads a newspaper headline that Eudora Welty has drowned in the Hook River and identifies with Welty to such an extent that she substitutes her own name in the headline. As she relays her dreams in letters to Mary, Carson is often chasing after clues—Where did the name "Hook River" come from? Why Welty?—instead of recognizing the emotional content of what she is saying. *I was holding you in my arms, embracing you, kissing you.* Hers is a wonderful and maddening kind of obliviousness. A constant blind spot. But this very nonchalance could suggest that recounting this dream does not serve as a shocking confession, but a replay of scenarios that have actually occurred with Mary. She feels no need to explain herself, or how they ended up entwined in embrace.

# Your Name

After she had been "fired" (her word) as Mary's patient, Carson sent a letter to her former doctor. Early that morning, she wrote, she opened her eyes with Mary on her mind. She loved her and wanted to tell her so but didn't want to wake her, so she waited to call her until eight, to say goodbye. Mary was flying to Spain with her then-husband, and Carson had been praying for her safety. The letter closes with Carson declaring that there isn't a single word loving enough to call her. I imagine Mary blushing when she receives this letter. I imagine her quietly delighted. Is this projection?

There isn't a clear explanation for why their therapy ended so abruptly. At some point, they seem to have just turned off the tape recorder. They decided to embark on a new relationship. "Therapy went marvelously well," Carson writes in *Illumination*, "and in less than a year, she discharged me as a patient. We have become devoted friends, and I cannot imagine life without our love and friendship." Ah, "friendship."

All the materials Mary saved are in Carson's voice (tapes, letters) or refer to legal battles following her death. Mary was careful to eliminate her own voice from the archive. Searching for Mary in her own words, trying to understand how she interpreted her relationship with Carson, I found myself—virtually—back in the McCullers papers at the Harry Ransom Center where I'd begun, just a few folders away from the Annemarie letters. From Santa Fe I ordered scans of Mary's letters from an intern, a reincarnation of me. They took two months to arrive, and when they did I couldn't bear to read them. After all that waiting, I was afraid. What if they somehow destroyed what I was working on? What if, in my desire to offer a version of Carson that I understood, in an effort to feel my own experience validated, I had manufactured the whole love story?

The letters are filled with mundane travel details—they wrote to each other only when one of them was out of town. They describe sites and visits and meals and hotels, and, in Mary's words, "missing, missing." Mary went to England in 1960 and sent Carson a telegram on arrival, another when she received the flowers Carson had sent her.

*JULY 28 1960 IT IS SO BEAUTIFUL. MARY.*

*AUG 9 1960 MUCH LOVE MARY*

*AUG 10 1960 THE BEAUTY OF FLOWERS FROM
MY BEST FRIEND ENCIRCLES US*

*LOVE MARY*

She also sent a letter back, enclosing a sprig of heather that
the archive scanned along with the page.

> *Caledonian Hotel, Edinburgh. Wed. My best friend
> has sent me flowers, before which, if she could see them,
> she would remain silent. No one could describe their
> beauty. Each day I wear a different colored rose. They
> are so radiant with a sturdy livingness that I can't
> believe that they will ever perish . . . I enclose some
> heather from me to you. MMDM Mary*

Mary mentions how much she misses her cats back home
in Nyack and above all encourages Carson to take care of
herself and stay healthy.

> *Tues night. Thank you for staying put and being. I
> know you promised to take especial care of yourself and
> I know you keep your word. So I do not worry. You
> and I shall have a great deal of fun living over this past
> week. It overflows. I prayed 'your prayer' by name last
> Sunday at a service at Westminister [sic] Abbey. Never
> have I heard such a choir. And I paused by the 3 Brontë
> sisters—"courage to endure"*

*There is such a sense of presence—almost every-where. There is no beginning—no end—even to this note. MMDM Mary.*

On another sheet, I find a clue to what Mary might have prayed at Westminster:

*Oh God, whose other name is Love,*
*Take the radiance and energies of Carson's love, which surrounds my days, and return them to her in full measure, increased by the love I have for her so that she stands illuminated and comforted. Give her the grace to express the essence of this abundance of loveliness in her life and in her work. Bless her and keep her. Amen.*

# Forensics

I approach all of Carson's materials—the clothes, the letters, the transcripts, the stories—so cautiously, in my own way, trying not to disturb anything. Though to some readers it might seem as if I ride roughshod over the versions of history with which we've grown comfortable; that I am invading a story that is not mine. But the materials, the records themselves, I approach as if they were crime scenes. It's the archivist in me. I seek to re-create things exactly as they were when I found them, as I found them. I try to show the whole approach, the materials and the gaps and the precise place and state I am in when I'm looking. Perhaps it is because I am approaching the dead. Approaching the beloved? I feel that if I can show my relationship to the materials, then others will see what I see.

While cataloging the final installment of David Foster Wallace's papers at the Ransom Center in 2012, I had a desperate need to feel cautious. This collection was a major purchase for the center. I wrote in an essay, "I begin with a delicacy that is paralyzing. I fear getting anything out of order, out of place. I fear removing the rubber bands, the paper clips, the numbered Post-it notes. I'm distinctly aware that if I mess up, if I lose the order, the order is lost. This is a tender operation." I realize now that I keep rewriting that one essay in different settings, trying to process those same feelings: loss, access, touch, erasures. I started working at the archive not long after a major archival scandal: Maria Bustillos published an article in *The Awl* in 2011 using the handwritten annotations in Wallace's book collection, specifically his collection of so-called "self-help" books. These notes reflected his struggles with mental illness and made mention of his mother. From the buzz around the building, I learned that these revelations were so upsetting to Wallace's family, they asked to pull some of the books they had sold to the Ransom Center from Wallace's library collection. The center agreed and rehoused those books in sealed boxes, separate from the rest, refusing researchers access to them. In my first months as an intern, writing my MA thesis on Wallace—pre-Carson—I stood for hours in the aisle where his personal library is housed, reading the books he read (the unrestricted ones) and reading his annotations. There is a liveness, a presence to reading, and I took comfort in this sense of vitality, of sharing an intellectual project with the dead. Library books, especially annotated ones, or ones with page corners creased, or with notes or bookmarks or other ephemera tucked into them, have given me this same feeling, this reprieve from loneliness, since I was a kid. Someone else was here.

Processing the last installment of Wallace's papers, his drafts and journals and endless floppy discs from his final, unfinished book, *The Pale King*, I grappled again with the problems of censorship. I had to flag any mention of home addresses, phone numbers, and email addresses that appeared in the collection so that the real archivists could remove them, preventing any future researchers from having access to private information about Wallace's friends and family members. These redactions seemed reasonable enough to me. No need to give DFW-hounds permission to stalk. But I was also instructed to flag instances where something "inappropriate" relating to Wallace's family members might appear. I assume this was a strategy to avoid future publications that might upset the family or the Wallace estate. Reading through the papers, it soon became difficult to discern what might comprise "inappropriate" or "upsetting" information—Wallace's narration of his own depression? Fictional representations of difficult family encounters? How was I to tell from the drafts and scattered notes what was fiction and what wasn't? In the end, I flagged only one page, and I don't know if the note was removed from the collection or not. It still forms a knot in my stomach to remember doing it.

Biography and its presumptions have bothered me for some time. Sometimes I think this project is an attempt at reparations (a failed one, in all likelihood): for my complicity in censorship at the archive, for my own closeted years, I am determined to shed light, to expose even those

things that are difficult about a writer's life. To track the
rewritings, the omissions, the revisions. Though I wonder,
constantly, what I might be omitting, revising, censoring.
What I am unable to see or let be seen. About Carson, and
about myself.

# Expurgation

The impulse to shed light collides with the collector's impulse, the need to gather up all the details. In Lorenza Foschini's book-length encounter with Marcel Proust's overcoat, her interest in a single article of clothing leads her to the story of a passionate collector who sought to salvage Proust from his own family—particularly his sister-in-law, Marthe—and their acts of censorship. I can't help but hear echoes of Carson's story in everything I read these days.

Foschini writes, "Proust's homosexuality surrounded him like an invisible and insurmountable wall. His family's unwillingness to understand this led to a history of silences that mutated into rancor. This in turn was transformed into acts of vandalism—papers destroyed, furniture abandoned." She explains the motive behind the destruction later in the book. "What mattered to [Marthe] was to remove all traces of indecency liable to expose the family name to shame and disgrace. In this spirit of vengeance, Marcel Proust's love letters were destroyed, as well as reams of his worldly correspondence, and most egregiously, innumerable drafts and working notes for his great masterwork."

"Indecency" could easily have motivated Mary to destroy papers pertaining to Carson. The "indecency" of their relationship (Mary was, after all, religious), the breach of doctor/patient roles, the threat to Mary's reputation as a therapist. As with Proust, as with so many queer writers and artists, there is no way to know fully what has been lost or destroyed. It is only possible to let absence speak.

# Lies, Secrets, and Silence

To read Carson's letters and therapy transcripts after reading the biographies and to continue to hear from strangers that Carson was not a lesbian, did not have a relationship with Mary, is unnerving. These flat-out lies are spoken as correctives, attempts to purify the record. But to know that Carson was a lesbian, to some extent, is to open up all of history: everyone may have been lesbian, no matter what the marriages or the records show. What freedom, what abundance live, in this realization.

While Carson was in Ireland in 1967, her very last trip abroad, visiting John Huston, who directed the film of *Reflections in a Golden Eye* with Marlon Brando and Elizabeth Taylor, Mary wrote her:

> *Tues PM. A part of my heart rose with you into the skies and disappeared over the Atlantic. Use it to enjoy and bring it back soon. Mary.*

JENN SHAPLAND

On the eve of Carson's return, Mary drew two fireplaces on the first page of her letter:

*Saturday. Fires burning day and night in both homes to light your return. MMDM*

These late years are represented by fewer letters. Perhaps Carson had run out of things to say, or perhaps she finally had someone she could talk to.

# Myth Mania

Mary annotated and saved letters pertaining to Carson in a filing cabinet in her home. She marked a paragraph in a letter from Robert Lantz, one of Carson's agents, in 1970, three years after her death. Lantz writes that it is less important to him that a biography offer a "literary evaluation" of Carson and her work. Rather, he longs for a version that presents "the living, extraordinary, unique, incredible lady" and "this fantastic tale of gallantry," emphasizing Mary's role in such a book's creation: "we will all have to help because we were the people who knew her and to some degree understood her." Whatever book Mary wanted—and certainly she didn't write it herself, though she is helping write this one—she did not seem especially interested in Lantz's mission to recover the "living, extraordinary, unique, incredible lady." More than immortalization, he seems to strive for resurrection. Roland Barthes's "The Death of the Author" clearly never made its way into Lantz's hands. I wonder, too, what "tale of gallantry" he's talking about here: Carson's ability to live and write in the face of illness? Mary's heroic caretaking of Carson at the end of her life?

I imagine his request did not sit well with Mary. Writing after the publication of Carr's biography *The Lonely Hunter*, Mary tells the young biographer Margaret Sullivan, "Carr's book on Carson should not trouble you because her reach was for notoriety. Your book will be a quiet study of Carson's work and its worth." The control Mary tries to assert over Sullivan's writing project feels to me, as a writer, strangling. And not exactly feminist, either, to tell her to write a "quiet study"—does that mean dull? Academic? A study that sticks to a version of Carson's life as told solely through her fiction? If that's the case, I start to wonder if Mary ever read Carson's books. They are, in my opinion, anything but quiet.

Lantz expresses his hope that "the right biographer" might extract from Mary "the details of the story of the many illnesses, the many operations, the many triumphs" that marked Carson's life.

Lantz wants the story of Carson's illness, or so he says, appealing to Mary's medical expertise. And she did leave behind the timeline of Carson's "Activities and Illnesses." But I find Boots's timeline, though less detailed, to be more poignant. After nearly every surgery—ten surgeries on her left hand, one to remove her right breast—and each hospitalization, he notes, *Mary was there.*

Lantz envisioned Mary as the person to serve as this mythical "right biographer" for Carson. His "secret hope" was that Mary might "write it all down" so that Carson's story could be seen through Mary's eyes, "not only with [her] medical understanding but with [her] remarkable love and devotion to Carson." Without saying or necessarily knowing anything about their relationship, Lantz makes it clear that he knows Mary was more than a doctor, more than a friend. It is this status that Mary refused to claim after Carson's death, keeping her notes and her records, but giving no details of her life with Carson to anyone. Withholding is a means of possession.

For a long time, I didn't read biographies, especially not biographies of writers. I couldn't stand the way they labored to establish some kind of one-to-one correlation between the random events of a person's life and her writing. Biographers broke into the house and rearranged the furniture to their liking. A few weeks after we started dating, Chelsea loaned me her well-worn copy of *Edie*, an oral history of Edie Sedgwick, Andy Warhol's superstar, by Jean Stein. As I read, sinking down into the bathtub where I spent much of my last year of graduate school, my idea of biography as a form shifted. I began to see just how many ways a person's life might be told. Stein crafts a narrative entirely out of other people's words. It encompasses the contradicting opinions and stories about its subject's life without trying to reconcile them. You can tell that some of the speakers are exaggerating, or trying to conceal something that perhaps the very next person will let out of the bag. It's juicy. It's alive. And unlike so many other biographies I've read, it feels true to life. Not true, whatever that means. But it does justice to the strangeness of memory, the unpredictability of human relationships, and it gives the lie to any instinct to impose a narrative rationale on unconnected events.

I began to wonder if that same principle Stein relies on—putting other voices into conversation to create an individual's story—could also have room for the author herself.

Carson read and recorded some of her work with Stein in 1958. Stein writes of her own sensitivity to the task of recovering another's voice:

> [Carson] seemed tormented by the ordeal ahead, and I almost wished that I hadn't suggested the project to her. During the reading I felt that she could hardly bear to communicate with her unknown audience. Later on I spent hours and hours splicing the tapes, eliminating her long pauses . . . even pulling syllables together. Looking back now, I think that it was dishonest to distort the way in which she expressed herself. But there remains untouched one shattering moment in which Miss McCullers broke down sobbing as she read the part of Frankie in a passage from *The Member of the Wedding.*

Stein's Carson is fragile but expressive. As a biographer, Stein is concerned about what she might be editing out, how she has spliced the voice of another.

# Recognition

After meeting with Floria Lasky, Carson's lawyer, to talk about the estate, Mary wrote a note to herself: "Floria et al see me as C's faithful doctor who was useful to her. C had to use everything & everyone. Yet, they want everything of meaning C ever did, said, or gave to me. Without acknowledging that C only did that if that person meant something to her. Problem: In Carson's eyes I was of significance. In their eyes I'm not." Reading little handwritten scraps alongside Mary's long-winded exchanges with Carson's lawyers, Rita, and the estate over her personal belongings allows me to see Mary not so much as a censoring, protecting possessor of Carson's legacy, but as someone who wanted somehow to be included in that legacy—acknowledged. She just didn't know how she might occupy that role without also outing herself, throwing her psychiatric practice, maybe even her faith, into question in the process.

When Margaret Sullivan, who began her biography of Carson while the author was still alive, asks to interview Mary after Carson's death, Mary writes back, "I doubt if I will ever be able to talk to you or anyone about Carson now or perhaps ever." This was 1971, four years after Carson's death. Sullivan presses further, in 1975, asking basic, factual questions: "Who signed the certificate and what was the cause of death? Is this on file anywhere? Also was an autopsy performed and is this on file? Was the early rheumatic fever diagnosis borne out or would it be? I know nothing of the time or circumstance except the poem you read me—I should not ask you to go through the painful experience again but my biography must come to its close. Forgive me." Mary does not respond to Sullivan, but asks her lawyer to do so. "Please respect the Doctor's wishes," he writes.

Sullivan can't let it go. She writes Mary again, defensively. She insists she "only asked the questions any competent biographer would have to ask." Two years later, when Sullivan asks Mary if she and her mother can come visit, Mary agrees but reiterates her wish to say nothing about Carson. "Time has made it abundantly clear that my public role in Carson's life was that of a physician." This statement raises many questions of its own, which Mary will never answer. How has time's passing clarified her role? Why specify "public"? Why "physician," rather than therapist? But perhaps most perplexingly: Why include these letters, along with the therapy transcripts and all the other documents of her nonpublic role in Carson's life, in the set of papers she donated and made available to the public upon her death in 2013?

And here is where I come in, waving my rainbow flag. I think I know why she made this public—in fact, it's very clear to me. Queer people have much to contribute to our collective knowledge of secrecy and its effects, though in this case it takes a queer ear, a familiarity with the interior of a closeted relationship, to hear it. Love must be public, shared. If you keep it to yourself, it doesn't really exist; it has no practical use in the world. Mary knew this, on some level. She longed to be recognized, if only by the lawyers in charge of Carson's estate. But she retreated after Carson was gone. She bought Carson's house, but she did not speak about her. She internalized her love and grief, despite the fact that, while Carson was alive, the two were quite publicly a couple. Friends wrote letters to "Carson and Mary," invited them to visit as a unit. Carson may not have consistently called herself a lesbian, or called herself anything, but she never denied her love for women. She never hid. After Carson died, they both went into the closet Carson had refused to occupy during her lifetime. Mary closed the door behind them.

In Columbus, the walls of Carson's house are covered in photos: most are of family, friends, Reeves. In the front room that used to be her bedroom is a single framed black-and-white photo of Carson and Mary, both looking down.

This is the only photo of Mary in the house. Unlike the timeline in the living room, this photo has no caption or wall text attached to it. But I recognize Mary instantly. They have identical haircuts.

# The Silencing Force

Margaret Sullivan never finished her book.

# Proximity

When I mention her name, most people don't recognize it, or they mistake her for someone else. I have withstood lengthy plot summaries of Flannery O'Connor stories remembered from high school English, mentions of how much the person I am talking to loved *No Country for Old Men*—Carson McCullers as Cormac McCarthy. When people don't recognize her name, I feel the need to mention that her books were well-known in her time, best sellers, that were made into movies and Broadway plays. Elizabeth Taylor! I add. But when the person does know Carson's work, they reply to my mention of her name with a look, a sort of swoon. *Isn't she wonderful?* I am never sure how to answer this; yes, I am writing a book about her? *I love her,* they say, as if this is possible. As I grew closer to Carson through research, it became more and more obvious that I was not alone in my sense of possession, of being possessed.

Everyone had a claim to lay, an attachment to prove. Everybody wanted a piece of her, including me. Eileen Myles:

On Thompson Street I lived on the same floor as
Carson McCullers, at a different time, but still just
a digit away. I was reading her bio in bed. I'm there
with a hangover, the sheets and the curling smoke
from my cigarette looming over the hidden ashtray
making a toy town and suddenly I read that she was
my neighbor. You know like in 1956. I walk out
the door in my underwear and I'm standing there
staring at hers. It was better than going to her grave,
and my pure intention protected me because I was
practically naked.

I hope my pure intention protects me, but as yet I cannot
identify, let alone articulate, what that intention might be.
I am having trouble letting go.

At what point, I wonder, will I again be able to watch a
movie or read anything about the twentieth century without framing it by the events of her life: Was that before or
after 1958? Before or after Mary?

# Myopia

Writing in late August 1974, Boots admits to his partiality and bias when writing his notes on Carson's life: "My own motives in making available these notes are open to question. Human motives are never wholly unselfish. But I hope I am not guilty of cover-up. We've had enough of that lately." I don't know what cover-up in particular he refers to—Mary's suppression of her relationship with Carson? Rita's suppression of information about herself? Everyone's collective family suppression of Carson's alcoholism and its effects on her already ill body? I rifle through all the possibilities I can think of until it dawns on me: *he's talking about Watergate.*

# September 29, 1967

Carson died, after forty-seven days in a coma. Judson Memorial Church in Greenwich Village, where Carson wanted her funeral held, was not available for her service. One of Gertrude Stein's plays was being performed there that day. The church was a venue for experimental theater and dance, hosting performers like Trisha Brown and Yvonne Rainer throughout the 1960s. The minister Carson chose, Reverend Howard Moody, was a well-known civil rights advocate. He offered a graveside service, attended by Mary, Rita, Boots, Marielle Bancou, Janet Flanner, Truman Capote, Wystan Hugh Auden, Gypsy Rose Lee, and Ethel Waters.

# September 29, 2016

I received my invitation to Yaddo after several months on the waiting list.

# Love and Winter

Carson and Mary communicated in poems: Rilke, Eliot, Dickinson. In February 1958, a year after their first meeting, Carson sent Mary an Emily Dickinson poem, typed with her own spellings and punctuation, apparently from memory:

*After great pain a formal feeling comes*
*The nerves sit ceremonious as tombs*
*The stiff heart questions, was it he that bore?*
*And yesterday or centuries before?*
*The feet mechanical go round in a wooden way*
*Of ought or nought or air, regardless grown*
*As qwartz, contentment, like a stone.*
*This is the hour of lead, remembered if outlived.*
*As freezing persons recollect the snow*
*First chill, then stupor, then the letting go*

To Mary, she writes that she had spent many years in the "eerie chill" and the "stupor," and that it was a lifelong battle for her to finally let go.

# The Dead

Maybe Mary was right: she didn't owe anyone Carson's, or her own, story. The biographers and lawyers coming after her, telling her that she needed to "share" Carson with the world, wanting so much from her: they were nothing but vultures, greedy for a connection to something that was never theirs. Maggie Nelson writes, "Jane is, after all, quite dead. We're talking about what the living need, or what the living imagine the dead need, or what the living imagine the dead would have wanted were they not dead. But the dead are the dead. Presumably they have finished with wanting." I don't know what Carson wanted or what Mary wanted. I don't know what the director wanted when he told me they weren't romantically involved. I think I know what I wanted, though, from Carson: recognition. A rendering of my own becoming. A love story I could believe.

# Dream

On the one hand, the transcripts and session letters come from early in Carson and Mary's relationship. They document a specific period of several months, premised on therapy and a patient speaking to her doctor. On the other hand, they are remarkable and unique: a record of Carson's falling in love, her processing and coming to terms with that love and, along the way, with her whole life of loves, especially for women, and her failed marriages. We watch her emerge from the lonely cave she had conscribed herself to, and walk painfully, honestly, into Mary's arms and presumably heart. I am presuming this. I believe in it. Not to believe in it, I think, is to reject all other documents of love as false, imperfect. If this isn't love I don't know what is. Or care.

# Note to Self

"Mail back Carson's keys."

# Euphemisms

To her husband, whom she married twice, Carson called her woman lovers "imaginary friends." Her biographers called them traveling companions, good friends, roommates, close friends, dear friends, obsessions, crushes, special friends. I'm over it. I, for one, am weary of the refusal to acknowledge what is plainly obvious, plainly wonderful. Call it love.

# Acknowledgments

Thank you, Bill Clegg, this book's earliest champion, Emma Komlos-Hrobsky, its fiercest supporter, and Masie Cochran, for seeing it through to the finish line. Thank you, Meg Storey, Rachel Warren, Jakob Vala, Elizabeth De-Meo, Molly Templeton, Yashwina Canter, Nanci McCloskey, Rob Spillman, Elissa Schappell, and every soul at Tin House and the Tin House Writers Workshop, especially my friends Thomas Ross and Lance Cleland. Thank you, Win McCormack, for taking a risk. For guidance through turbid legal waters, thank you Ellis Levine, tireless researchers Liz and Peter Komlos-Hrobsky, and Chris Kaiser, my lifelong legal counsel.

Thank you, Nick Norwood, David Owings, the Columbus State University Archives, and the Carson McCullers Center for Writers and Musicians; Rick Watson and the staff at the Harry Ransom Center, especially the interns; Anne McKenna and the University of Wisconsin Press; Yaddo, Tal Nadan, and the Brooke Russell Astor Reading Room

JENN SHAPLAND

for Rare Books & Manuscripts at the New York Public
Library; the Rubenstein Library at Duke University; the
Swiss Literary Archives at the Swiss National Library; Ver-
mont Studio Center; and Ucross Foundation.

Thank you, Rhiannon Marge Goad, for being a friend;
thanks, Laura Wallace and Katie Loughmiller, for reading
and rereading. Thank you to my family.

Thank you, Chelsea Weathers, for our life.

# Sources

## ARCHIVAL COLLECTIONS

Annemarie Schwarzenbach Estate. Swiss National Library Literary Archives. Bern, Switzerland.

Carson McCullers Collection 1924–1976. Harry Ransom Center. University of Texas, Austin, TX.

Carson McCullers Papers, 1941–1995. Rubenstein Library. Duke University, Durham, NC.

Davis Foster Wallace Papers. Harry Ransom Center. Austin, TX.

Dr. Mary E. Mercer/Carson McCullers Collection. Columbus State University Archives. Columbus, GA.

Jordan Massee—Carson McCullers Collection. Columbus State University Archives. Columbus, GA.

Mary E. Mercer Collection of Carson McCullers-Mary Tucker Correspondence, 1959–1976. Rubenstein Library, Duke University, Durham, NC.

JENN SHAPLAND

Virginia Spencer Carr Papers, 1967–2009. Rubenstein Library, Duke University. Durham, NC.

Yaddo Records, 1870–1980. New York Public Library, New York, NY.

## WORKS CONSULTED

Adkins, Judith. "'These People Are Frightened to Death' Congressional Investigations and the Lavender Scare." *Prologue* 48.2, 2016.

Als, Hilton. "Unhappy Endings: The Collected Carson McCullers." *The New Yorker* December 3, 2001.

Blumenkranz, Carla. "Deeply and Mysteriously Implicated: Communist Sympathies, FBI Informants, and Robert Lowell at Yaddo." *Poetry Foundation*, 2006.

Carr, Virginia Spencer. *The Lonely Hunter: A Biography of Carson McCullers.* Athens, GA: University of Georgia Press, 2003.

Castle, Terry. *The Apparitional Lesbian: Female Homosexuality and Modern Culture.* New York: Columbia University Press, 1993.

Chauncey, George, Jessica Shatan, Archie Ferguson, and Vicki Gold Levi. *Gay New York: Gender, Urban Culture, and the Making of the Gay Male World, 1890–1940.* New York: Basic, 1994.

Cohen, Lisa. *All We Know: Three Lives.* New York: Farrar, Straus and Giroux, 2012.

260

Dillon, Millicent. *A Little Original Sin: The Life and Work of Jane Bowles.* New York: Holt, Rinehart and Winston, 1981.

————. *Out in the World: Selected Letters of Jane Bowles 1935–1970.* Santa Barbara, CA: Black Sparrow Press, 1985.

Duncan, Isadora. *My Life.* New York: Liveright, 2013.

Evans, Oliver Wendell. *The Ballad of Carson McCullers: A Biography.* New York: Coward-McCann, 1965.

————. *Carson McCullers: Her Life and Work.* London: Peter Owen, 1965.

Faderman, Lillian. *Odd Girls and Twilight Lovers: A History of Lesbian Life in Twentieth-Century America.* New York: Penguin, 1991.

Ferrante, Elena, and Ann Goldstein. *Frantumaglia: A Writer's Journey.* New York: Europa Editions, 2016.

Flanner, Janet. *Darlinghissima: Letters to a Friend.* Edited by Natalia Danesi Murray. New York: Random House, 1985.

Flanner, Janet, and Irving Drutman. *Paris Was Yesterday, 1925–1939.* London: Virago, 2011.

Foschini, Lorenza. *Proust's Overcoat.* New York: Ecco, 2010.

Frankel, Noralee. *Stripping Gypsy: The Life of Gypsy Rose Lee.* New York: Oxford University Press, 2010.

Goldberg, Natalie. *Writing Down the Bones.* Boulder: Shambhala, 1986.

Gooch, Brad. *Flannery: A Life of Flannery O'Connor.* New York: Little, Brown, 2009.

Gornick, Vivian. *The Situation and the Story: The Art of Personal Narrative.* New York: Farrar, Straus and Giroux, 2002.

Gussow, Mel. *Edward Albee: A Singular Journey.* New York: Simon and Schuster, 1999.

Hamer, Emily. *Britannia's Glory.* London: Cassell, 1996.

Hammond, Harmony. *Lesbian Art in America: A Contemporary History.* New York: Rizzoli, 2000.

Hemon, Aleksandar. "Stop Making Sense, or How to Write in the Age of Trump." *Village Voice* January 2017.

Highsmith, Patricia. *Nothing That Meets the Eye: The Uncollected Stories of Patricia Highsmith.* New York: W.W. Norton, 2003.

Highsmith, Patricia. Pseudonym Claire Morgan. *The Price of Salt;* or *Carol.* New York: Dover Publications, 1952.

Huston, John. *Reflections in a Golden Eye* (film). Warner Brothers, 1967. DVD.

Johnston, Jill. "Fictions of the Self in the Making." *New York Times Book Review* April 1993.

Kaiser, Charles. *The Gay Metropolis: The Landmark History of Gay Life in America.* New York: Grove, 2007.

Lahr, John. *Tennessee Williams: Mad Pilgrimage of the Flesh.* New York: W.W. Norton, 2014.

Laing, Olivia. *The Trip to Echo Spring: On Writers and Drinking.* New York: Picador, 2014.

Lawson, Richard. "The Bittersweet Beauty of Adam Rippon." *Vanity Fair* 2018.

Leyda, Jay. *The Years and Hours of Emily Dickinson.* New Haven, CT: Yale University Press, 1970.

Lorde, Audre. *Zami: A New Spelling of My Name.* Berkeley: Crossing Press, 1982.

Malcolm, Janet. *Forty-One False Starts: Essays on Artists and Writers.* London: Granta, 2014.

_____. *In the Freud Archives.* London: Granta, 2012.

_____. *The Silent Woman: Sylvia Plath and Ted Hughes.* London: Granta, 2012.

McCullers, Carson. *The Ballad of the Sad Café and Other Stories.* Boston: Houghton Mifflin, 1951.

_____. *Clock Without Hands.* Boston: Houghton Mifflin, 1961.

_____. *The Member of the Wedding*. Boston: Houghton Mifflin, 1946.

_____. *Reflections in a Golden Eye*. Boston: Houghton Mifflin, 1941.

McCullers, Carson, and Carlos L. Dews. *Illumination and Night Glare: The Unfinished Autobiography of Carson McCullers*. Madison: University of Wisconsin Press, 1999.

McCullers, Carson, and Rita Smith. *The Mortgaged Heart: Previously Uncollected Writings*. Boston: Houghton Mifflin, 1971.

McGee, Micki. *Yaddo: Making American Culture*. New York: Columbia University Press, 2008.

Milford, Nancy. *Zelda: A Biography*. New York: Harper and Row, 1970.

Myles, Eileen. *Chelsea Girls*. New York: Ecco, an Imprint of HarperCollins, 2015.

_____. *The Importance of Being Iceland: Travel Essays in Art*. Los Angeles: Semiotext(e), 2009.

_____. *Inferno: A Poet's Novel*. New York: OR, 2016.

Nealon, Christopher. *Foundlings: Lesbian and Gay Historical Emotion before Stonewall*. Durham: Duke University Press, 2001.

Nelson, Maggie. *The Argonauts*. Minneapolis, MN: Graywolf, 2016.

_____. *The Red Parts: Autobiography of a Trial*. Minneapolis, MN: Graywolf, 2016.

Newton, Esther. *Cherry Grove, Fire Island: Sixty Years in America's First Gay and Lesbian Town*. Boston: Beacon, 1995.

Plimpton, George. *Truman Capote: In Which Various Friends, Enemies, Acquaintances, and Detractors Recall His Turbulent Career*. New York: Anchor, 1998.

Quinn, Susan. *Eleanor and Hick: The Love Affair That Shaped a First Lady*. New York: Penguin, 2016.

Rausing, Sigrid. *Do You Remember*. London: Granta, 2014.

Savigneau, Josyane. *Carson McCullers: A Life*. Boston: Houghton Mifflin, 2001.

Schenkar, Joan. *The Talented Miss Highsmith: The Secret Life and Serious Art of Patricia Highsmith*. New York: St. Martin's, 2010.

Schulman, Sarah. "White Writer." *The New Yorker* October 2016.

Schwarzenbach, Annemarie, and Dominique Laure. Miermont. *La Mort En Perse*. Paris: Payot Et Rivages, 2008.

Sears, James. *Edwin and John: A Personal History of the American South*. Hoboken: Taylor & Francis, 2009.

Stein, Jean. Edited with George Plimpton. *Edie: An American Biography*. New York: Knopf, 1982

Stein, Marc. *Encyclopedia of Lesbian, Gay, Bisexual, and Transgender History in America.* New York: Charles Scribner's Sons/ Thomson/Gale, 2004.

Tippins, Sherill. *February House.* London: Pocket, 2006.

Weiss, Andrea. *In the Shadow of the Magic Mountain: The Erika and Klaus Mann Story.* Chicago: University of Chicago Press, 2008.

Wilson, Andrew. *Beautiful Shadow: A Life of Patricia Highsmith.* New York: Bloomsbury, 2003.

Wineapple, Brenda. *Genêt: A Biography of Janet Flanner.* Omaha: University of Nebraska Press, 1992.

# Queering the Archive

SARAH NEILSON INTERVIEWS JENN SHAPLAND

*Your book is both a memoir about your own life and a biography of McCullers. You don't separate your story from hers—the narrative threads become increasingly entwined. How did you choose this structure?*

I knew immediately *My Autobiography of Carson McCullers* wasn't going to be a linear narrative, because no matter what I tried, the story kept wrapping back around and folding in on itself. The book has eighty chapters, but it's fewer than three hundred pages long. These short chapters gave me a way to record that movement without trying to strap it into a clear trajectory. When I first started writing, the sentences came to me in these sections, often in direct response to an archival object I encountered. I was inspired to write this way by Lydia Davis, who always lets her titles do really important work, and who lets even small insights stand on their own on the page as a story. There are other writers who work this way, but she's the one that I feel kinship with.

*How did your background as an archivist affect the book?*

There is something archival about this book, and in my writing practice in general. I want to record not just the thought, but also where I'm having it and what the details are of the day that gave rise to the thought, all that context, or what an archivist would call metadata. Of course any archivist would say these chapters are nothing like actual archival entries, but I think there's a relationship: both come from a drive to record as much as possible, to avoid losing any information that might be useful later on. I work as an archivist for an artist in New Mexico, and this continues to be my daily task: how can we capture all of what this photo or artwork or letter tells us in the logical space of language?

*Closets are an interesting facet of* My Autobiography. *The metaphorical queer closet is itself a site of archival material, as are literal closets. How did these archival discoveries impact your understanding of McCullers?*

I love clothes, and I make clothes (and had my own ill-conceived clothing line, Agnes, for a spell). I also worked with clothing and personal effects as an intern at the Harry Ransom Center. Clothes are so personal, so mundane, so close to the body and the home, all of which is why these items drew me in to Carson's story. Clothes also say so much about how a person presents herself. A really important part of queer history, and queer life-making, is looking at photographs, outfits, and finding personal icons.

I tried not to lean too hard on the metaphor of the closet in the book, but I like what you say about how the closet is its own archive, and this book is kind of rifling through it. Rather than limiting, I found the objects and documents in various archives to be freeing, to really open up the story and change the fixed narrative that was out there. All of the little cards that came with flowers Carson sent to Mary, that Mary saved. The objects kind of sing with meaning, and it felt like my job to translate that meaning into writing so that others who couldn't engage with them directly could access those stories.

*Speaking of the flowers and letters McCullers sent to Mary Mercer, you write about "evidence" of love in the book, that love "lives in the mundane. . . . But, of course, it leaves traces." In what ways is* My Autobiography *a love story?*

It tells my own love story, falling in love with my partner, Chelsea, which coincided with the research and writing of the book (we met in the archive where I found Carson's love letters from Annemarie). It's also about my own "love story" with Carson. I think my love for Carson as a writer and a person betrays itself in my obsession with getting her story right. I'm trying to understand her and make others understand her as I see her; it's a kind of love that is possessive. When I read something that feels inaccurate, that possessiveness comes out. And then there is the grand love story that I uncovered in Columbus, in the Mary Mercer papers, though I don't want to spoil anything. But I think that's the real love story of the book, and it's juicy.

*The book also has a bit of a ghost story element to it. There's a haunted-house vibe when you're staying in McCullers's former home. Then there's the ghost of her queer identity, which was erased by many of the people who told her story after she died. You even characterize yourself as a ghost in her house, deliberately remaining hidden to outsiders. This ties in with how McCullers's husband, Reeves, referred to her female crushes as "imaginary friends," effectively making them unreal. What is ghostly about the hidden or missing narratives of queer lives?*

Researching someone else's life so intensely—living in her childhood home, cataloging her clothing and objects, reading her letters and therapy transcripts, following her to the very haunted Yaddo—got me thinking about what it means to feel possessed, or haunted, and what it means to haunt or possess others. Carson's life was haunted by old loves and fears that all turned up in the transcripts of her therapy sessions with Mary in 1958. She's in her forties, but she's still talking about one particular night with Annemarie in her early twenties that haunts her, the violence of her abusive husband, and her mother's death. Her drinking haunts her, too, and in letters to Mary she's always promising to cut back. I suppose I see these as parts of her life that she struggled to reconcile, and a lot of it reads like a coming out process. She's slowly finding the language to integrate all of her experiences into an identity. What Reeves called "imaginary friends" were the deep loves of her life, and it seems that only in her later years, after Reeves was gone, could she start to claim them as significant and real.

Something people love to ask me is if I saw or encountered Carson's ghost while writing the book or living in her house. Um, no? I think what they're really asking is, "Did you have permission from Carson's spirit to write this? Do you have some kind of direct access to her truth?" And, honestly, if her ghost is around she's probably drunk at a party talking trash in the corner about Truman Capote, and I'm busy taking a bath and writing little notes to myself and taking naps. We didn't cross paths.

*You write about chronic illness and queerness as ways of being lonely in a world that erases or devalues both. How do chronic illness and queerness show up in the body, and how are they physically connected?*

I was coming to terms with both my chronic illness (POTS, which can cause extreme physical fatigue and frequent migraines) and with coming out as a lesbian during the period

I was writing this book. I realized that there was no way for me to live as a "healthy normal," that certain things about me made me emphatically different from how I thought I ought to be. As I learned how to be "out," to claim a queer identity in public and in writing, I began to notice how my illness was something I still tried to hide. Writing about it gave me a way to take something that is deeply personal and subjective—the physical experience of my own body—and make it into language, which also made it more real. Others could recognize and respond to it. There are deep connections between queerness and sickness. Both are often hidden or private; the word *sick* can mean physically ill, mentally ill, or somehow perverted. Both sexuality and illness arise from the physical body and can't be immediately known by others. They're feelings that are often hidden from ourselves.

*Right, and that's one reason queer lives often don't fit neatly into conventional biographical narratives. How did you think about genre as you were piecing together McCullers's story?*

I struggle with biography as a genre, because I'm deeply interested in life writing, but allergic to anything that starts with "So-and-so was born in 1946." Who is this third person claiming omniscience about someone else's life? Why must we begin with birth, which no one remembers, or with ancestors, and move chronologically? The written record about Carson tries to sandwich her into a conventional, straight biography, wherein a person is born, comes of age, marries, and dies. That's just not how her life went, or that's not a way to capture the really exciting stuff, like her relationships with women that happened while she was married, her getting divorced and remarrying and abandoning the same guy, living with the queer cadre at February House, meeting Mary Mercer in her forties and falling in love, coming of age late in life. Queer narratives are all over the place, and queer people frequently take a long time to figure shit out. They live many lives in the space of one life, often with different identities, genders, pronouns, bodies, and styles. Queer narratives demand new forms, and I would love to see more queer writing that fucks with all different genres and literary conventions.

*This interview originally appeared in* Bookforum's *online edition in February 2020.*

**JENN SHAPLAND** is a writer living in New Mexico. She won the 2019 Rabkin Foundation Award for art journalism, her essay "Finders, Keepers" won a 2017 Pushcart Prize, and she has a PhD in English from the University of Texas at Austin. *My Autobiography of Carson McCullers* was a finalist for the 2020 National Book Award in Nonfiction, and was longlisted for the 2021 Andrew Carnegie Medal for Excellence in Nonfiction.